W9-CDO-224

ORIOLE PARK BRANCH

DATE DUE   1-04

JUL 3 1 2004			
NOV 2 6 2004			
MAR 0 1 2005			

DEMCO 38-296

DORLING KINDERSLEY DK EYEWITNESS BOOKS

WITCHES &
MAGIC-MAKERS

"Happiness" amulet
from Palestine

Stereotypical
witch

Witch's
painted
spirit-bone

Tibetan
magical
ritual
dagger

Lucky
horseshoe

Holed "witch
stones"

Witch
bottle filled
with
colored
essence

Guatemalan
"trouble doll"

Magical
rosebuds

DK EYEWITNESS BOOKS

WITCHES &
MAGIC-MAKERS

Written by
DOUGLAS HILL

Photographed by
ALEX WILSON

Witch's
cauldron

Dorling Kindersley

Tibetan dance headdress

Wizard's staff

DK

Dorling Kindersley
LONDON, NEW YORK, DELHI,
JOHANNESBURG, MUNICH, PARIS and SYDNEY

For a full catalog, visit

DK www.dk.com

Project editor Roderick Craig
Art editor Ann Cannings
Assistant designer Iain Morris
Managing editor Gillian Denton
Managing art editor Julia Harris
Production Charlotte Traill
Picture research Sharon Southren
DTP designer Nicky Studdart

This Eyewitness ® Book has been conceived by
Dorling Kindersley Limited and Editions Gallimard

© 1997 Dorling Kindersley Limited
This edition © 2000 Dorling Kindersley Limited
First American edition, 1997

Published in the United States by Dorling Kindersley Publishing, Inc.
375 Hudson Street,
New York, New York 10014
6 8 10 9 7 5

Late Victorian
magic wand

Dorling Kindersley books are available at special discounts for bulk purchases for sales promotions or premiums. Special editions, including personalized covers, excerpts of existing guides, and corporate imprints can be created in large quantities for specific needs. For more information, contact Special Markets Dept., Dorling Kindersley Publishing, Inc., 95 Madison Ave., New York, NY 10016; Fax: (800) 600-9098

Modern
shamanic
feather fan

Library of Congress Cataloging-in-Publication Data
Hill, Douglas Arthur, (1935–)
Witches & magic-makers / written by Douglas Hill; photography by Alex Wilson.
p. cm. — (Eyewitness Books) Includes index.
Summary: Presents the practices, rituals, and roles of witches and magic-makers around the world and throughout history.
1. Witchcraft—Juvenile literature. [1. Witchcraft.] I. Wilson, Alex, ill. II. Title.
BF1566.H55   2000   133.4'3—dc20   96-42958
ISBN 0-7894-5879-9 (pb)
ISBN 0-7894-5878-0 (hc)

Color reproduction by
Colourscan, Singapore
Printed in China by
Toppan Printing Co. (Shenzhen) Ltd.

African charm
pouches

Authentic
witch's hat

Crystal ball

Witch's
saucepan for
making potions

Bay leaves – supposed to magically improve the memory

Contents

Lemon verbena – used by witches in healing infusions

Native American shaman's rattle

The art of magic

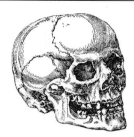

MORTAL REMAINS
Human skulls have often been kept and displayed like "museum pieces" by witches, wizards, and occult scholars. Such relics from the grave reminded the magic-makers and their clients of human mortality.

WITCHES HAVE ALSO been called "enchantresses" or even "weird sisters," while wizards have been "sorcerers" or "magicians." (We usually think of witches as women, yet there can be male witches; they were once called "warlocks.") But whatever we call them, one thing has always been true of them – they are *human magic-makers*. And not always evil magic: witches and wizards just as often use their craft for beneficial purposes. For that reason, through history, magic-makers were usually not feared but respected and revered – as the "wise ones," the priests and priestesses, the traditional healers, and also the historians and teachers who, as guardians of a community's time-honored lore and knowledge, passed it on to the next generation.

WICKED COOKS
This old German woodcut shows the common notion of witches as old hags making foul magic in their cauldron. Yet the image was mostly an invention by witch-hunters (pp. 22–23) to convince the public that witchcraft was wholly and utterly evil.

BUBBLE, BUBBLE
A typical witch's cauldron, once used by a local witch or "wise woman" in Devon, England. In the past, cauldrons like this were suspended in a fireplace and used as cooking pots in which a poor family's broth or stew might simmer. Now we associate cauldrons entirely with magic potions and "witches' brews."

WIRED UP
This human-like figure constructed of wire was made by a magic-maker during the 1930s in Brittany, France, probably for a spell aimed at a particular person. Usually, such a "hex doll" would be made of wax or clay, mixed with the victim's hair or nail clippings.

Rue

Lavender

GARDEN MAGIC
These three wild plants are among hundreds that might have been used by a wise woman in her healing remedies. Another magical remedy was the "rolling stone," which would have a spell cast on it, then be warmed in the oven and rolled gently over an afflicted part of the body to relieve discomfort.

Catnip

Wizards often wore skullcaps

WIZARDLY WISE
An instantly recognizable imaginary wizard, sporting long gray locks and a rich velvet robe decorated with magical symbols. He reads from a leatherbound volume, perhaps a *grimoire*, or spell book, reflecting his position, which is like that of a "tribal elder," with a deep and wide-ranging knowledge of secret lore.

HANDS OF SORCERY
These plaster casts of hands were found nailed to a tree trunk in rural France, and date to the 18th century. Each represents magical gestures; the one on the left was commonly thought to ward off evil magic.

WORD OF POWER
We think of "Abracadabra" as a word shouted by a stage magician, but it is in fact an ancient spell word from Biblical times, roughly meaning "begone!" Often inscribed on a triangle, it was a medieval charm against disease.

```
A
AB
ABR
ABRA
ABRAC
ABRACA
ABRACAD
ABRACADA
ABRACADAB
ABRACADABR
ABRACADABRA
```

IN THE RING
This 14th-century illustration shows a wizard (who is also a knight) standing in a typical "magic circle" of strange symbols written on the ground, in order to conjure spirits or cast a spell – no doubt a good one, since he is being watched by a friar.

Pentacle

SEAL OF WIZARDRY
This wax disk belonged to a famous wizard of Elizabethan times. It is inscribed with magical shapes, including a five-sided "pentacle" and a seven-pointed star, believed to provide powerful protective magic.

Stranger than fiction

BOOKS, FILMS, AND COMICS have given us fixed ideas of what witches and wizards look like. Witches are always ugly old hags with pointy hats, and wizards are old men with long white hair and spooky, hooded cloaks. Yet these descriptions would not be recognized by many people in different parts of the world, or in the past. They might have expected magic-makers to be strange-looking, dressed in outlandish costumes, perhaps even wearing masks, but never cackling hags or robed graybeards. And some people might think of a witch or wizard as looking completely ordinary, with only their special, secret knowledge of the magical arts setting them apart from the rest of their community.

Antlers represent the spirit of the animal

Yellow, symbol of the sun

Red, symbol of life

WITCH'S STEED
A traditional painted broom that once belonged to a Devon witch. Witches were thought to fly around on hoes and spades as well as brooms. The idea may have arisen out of ancient rites, where dancers used long-handled tools as hobbyhorses.

Green, symbol of growth

Blue, symbol of the sky

WIZARD STICK
A modern wizard's staff, its "natural magic" believed to come from its weirdly twisted form, the antlers, and the animal fur. Staffs might also be decorated with magical letters and cryptic "runes" (Nordic symbols).

CAVEMAN MAGIC
Found in France, this prehistoric cave painting depicts a figure wearing antlers and a tail – probably a shaman costumed for some kind of magical ceremony. It is the oldest-known image of a human magic-worker.

IN THE LABORATORY
This engraving shows a medieval alchemist looking very much like a wizard. The main aim of alchemists was to discover the "philosopher's stone," a substance they believed could guarantee eternal youth as well as change all materials to gold.

SADDLED UP
A male witch (who himself looks quite ordinary) riding a peculiar-looking animal to a witches' meeting. This image dates from the witch persecutions of the 1400s, when most witches were presented as monstrous and demonic.

EXOTIC MAGIC
In contrast to Western ideas of wizards, magic-workers from almost anywhere in Asia and Africa look more like these two village shamans and healers from Papua New Guinea, their faces and bodies painted.

TAKE A SEAT
This tree fungus from rural England is a charming example of local folklore surrounding witches. Called a "witch's seat," it was believed that a witch roaming the forest might perch on it for a rest (like a pixie on a toadstool).

WEIRD SISTER
The stock, familiar image of the "wicked witch" reflected in books and films, cartoons, and Halloween costumes all over Europe and the United States today – a hook-nosed old crone with warts on her beaky chin, long and cracked claw-like fingernails, and black, old-fashioned clothes. This stereotype dates back to olden times, when many poverty-stricken old women were accused, usually on the flimsiest evidence, of witchcraft.

Dry, cracked skin

GETTING TOGETHER
Three South African "shamanesses" and healers attending a conference in Johannesburg, dressed in splendidly colorful traditional costume and beaded headgear. They remind us that not all tribal magic-makers are male. These women play a respected and beneficial role in their communities, even today.

Black and rotten teeth

A hairy wart, a trademark of the stereotypical witch

Famous witches and wizards

HISTORY RECORDS THE names of a great many notable witches and wizards, good ones and evil ones, from ancient times to the present day. Many of these historical magic-makers actually did claim to possess the power of magic and other extraordinary abilities, and often gained their fame as professionals who (according to the legends that surround them) performed many amazing feats. For these great names, however, the labels "witch" or "wizard" were rarely used; they and their admirers usually preferred terms like "mystic" or "seer." On the other hand, some famous figures of the past are remembered as magic-makers because *others* called them witches or wizards – in order to accuse them of magical evildoing, out of fear, malice, or religious fervor, seeking to have them punished, even executed.

EVIL UNCOVERED
This illustration shows Apollonius of Tyana, a Greek wizard and prophet of the 1st century A.D. Here he magically reveals to one Menippus of Corinth the evil nature of his wife. Among Apollonius's alleged powers was the ability to speak with the dead (necromancy).

MYSTIC MATHEMATICIAN
This portrait is of the Greek philosopher and mystic Pythagoras (6th century B.C.), who made important discoveries in mathematics. He also taught mystic philosophy imported from Egypt. He believed that the soul could travel out of the body; one legend says that he has often reappeared in human form in later centuries.

MAGICAL MARTYR
The occult writings of Raymond Lully (1235–1316), a Spanish mystic and alchemist, drew the wrath of the Catholic Church. Later in his life he became more devout and was killed in North Africa trying to convert the Muslims.

POETIC WIZARDRY
The celebrated Roman poet Virgil (70–19 B.C.), author of the *Aeneid*, was later believed to have been a wizard by the people of Naples. One tale says that he made a magical brass fly that kept the town free of offensive insects.

STANDING ACCUSED

This portrait is of Joan of Navarre (1370–1437), Duchess of Brittany, who married Henry IV of England. When Henry was away fighting in France, her enemies at court accused her of seeking to harm the king through witchcraft. She was arrested and imprisoned for many years, but was later pardoned and reinstated.

SORCEROUS BRIBERY

This 15th-century painting shows the notorious 1st-century A.D. sorcerer Simon Magus offering money to the apostle Peter to "buy" his miracle-working power. In his time, Simon Magus was believed to be able to fly, change shape, and become invisible.

DANGEROUS DABBLING

This portrait is of Gilles de Rais (1404–40), a French baron who was said to be Europe's richest nobleman. His dabblings in alchemy and magic – and probably also the hatred and envy of his enemies – led to his being accused of devil-worship and abducting children, a crime for which he was burned at the stake. Not surprisingly, his property was confiscated and divided up among his rivals.

SCHOLARLY MAGIC

This 16th-century woodcut shows the famous German scholar Albertus Magnus (1193–1280). He was a bishop and philosopher as well as an alchemist and student of magic. His expertise included the "natural" magic properties of herbs and gemstones.

PROPHETIC WITCH

This satirical drawing shows the 15th-century Yorkshire witch Mother Shipton. Her powers were believed to include healing and spell-casting, while her "prophecies" seem to have foretold modern realities such as cars and airplanes.

OCCULT DANGERS

Heinrich Cornelius Agrippa (1486–1535) was one of the most famous occultists of his time, and his life demonstrates the dangers of such fame. Believed to have a demonic "familiar" spirit (pp. 38–39) and to be able to conjure up evil spirits, he was persecuted relentlessly by the Church authorities.

Behind the scenes

A historical catalog of magic-makers would show many more men than women. This is because men in the past could study to become scholars and practitioners of magic, and were free to seek public reputations and fame; but the majority of women who practiced magic and who were not wealthy aristocrats had to be content operating in more local or domestic spheres. Many genuine witches, or wise women, were probably quite happy to keep a low profile, as they could work without attracting the attention of those opposed to their craft.

TRAGIC END
This portrait is of Anne Boleyn (1507–36), the second of Henry VIII of England's six wives. When Henry tired of her because she could not produce an heir, he began the process of destroying her reputation by claiming that she had seduced him using witchcraft. She had a sixth finger on one hand, which was considered a sign of her being a witch. Henry later had her beheaded.

ALTERNATIVE MEDICINE MAN
The famed Swiss physician Paracelsus (1493–1541) was a practicing alchemist and magician. Although he spurned popular, frivolous sorceries, he admired the "healing magic" of herbs and minerals and held advanced "holistic" views on how the spirit, mind, and body affect one another.

Leatherbound wood case

IN A GLASS DARKLY
This obsidian "mirror," said to be imported from the Aztec civilization of ancient Mexico, belonged to Dr. John Dee (1527–1608), an astrologer and reputed magician who was a favorite of Queen Elizabeth I of England. He used the mirror for a form of divination similar to crystal-gazing.

CODED VERSES
This caricature depicts the renowned French healer, diviner, and occultist Nostradamus (1503–66). His cryptic, prophetic verses seem to foretell the French Revolution, the rise of Napoleon and Hitler, and the end of the world (in the 38th century).

SCOTS WITCH-HUNT
This woodcut depicts the "North Berwick witches," a group of men and women scandalously accused of witchcraft in 16th-century Scotland. On minimal evidence, they were condemned, tortured, and burned; they were said to have raised a storm in an attempt to drown the king, James I.

VICTIM OF THE FRENZY
This portrait is of Urbain Grandier, a 17th-century French priest, who was accused of witchcraft and tortured before being burned at the stake in Loudun – one of the most notorious cases of witch-frenzy in Europe.

HONORED SEER
This is the English diviner and astrologer William Lilly (1602–81), who was held in high regard by King Charles I. Astrology was then a serious subject for academic study; Lilly wrote just as seriously about magic and the art of conjuring spirits.

WIZARD OF ADVENTURE
This bust portrays the Italian adventurer Alessandro di Cagliostro (1743–95). He was said to possess psychic powers that enabled him to make a fortune in lotteries. As a diviner, healer, and wizard, he earned the disapproval of the Church and was finally imprisoned for life.

CON MAN
The 18th-century French alchemist, the Count of Saint-Germain, may be one of the famous frauds of magical history. Claiming that his powers had enabled him to live for 2,000 years, he acquired many wealthy and gullible clients.

QUEEN OF SPELLS
This portrait shows Caroline of Brunswick (1768–1821), queen to George IV of England. The story goes that because she felt neglected by her husband, she made a wax effigy of him, stuck pins and thorns into it, and melted it in a palace fireplace.

Witches in fiction

STORYTELLERS HAVE BEEN weaving tales of witchcraft and wizardry since before writing was invented, and magic-makers have captured the imagination throughout history. They are encountered in ancient legends and folktales, in stage dramas of every sort from slapstick comedies to grand opera, in children's stories, popular thrillers, and classic works of literature. And they remain as popular as ever today, in movies and even high-tech computer games.

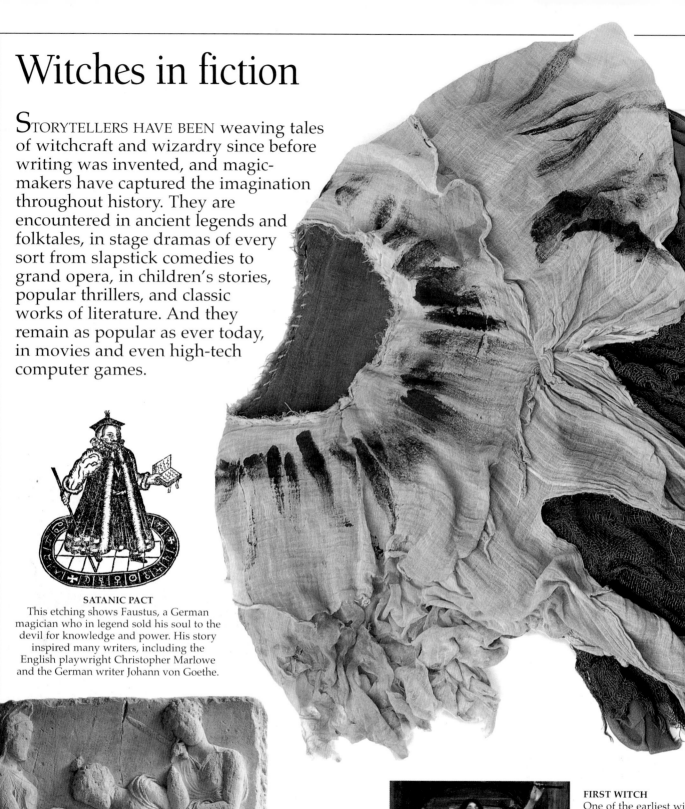

SATANIC PACT
This etching shows Faustus, a German magician who in legend sold his soul to the devil for knowledge and power. His story inspired many writers, including the English playwright Christopher Marlowe and the German writer Johann von Goethe.

MURDEROUS MAGIC
This 5th-century B.C. stone relief depicts the witch Medea (left), who in Greek mythology helped her husband, Jason, to capture the Golden Fleece. A tragic figure, she committed several murders, including those of her own children.

FIRST WITCH
One of the earliest witches in literature was Circe, who appears in the *Odyssey*. Homer's epic poem tells of the adventures of the Greek hero Odysseus on his journey home from the Trojan War. As depicted in this painting by John William Waterhouse (1849–1917), Circe turned Odysseus's friends into swine after they landed on her island. She also tried to get Odysseus to drink an evil magic potion. Fortunately, he managed to escape and restore his men to human form.

WIZARD'S FATE
The legendary Merlin, originally from Welsh mythology, became the mainstay of King Arthur's Round Table. In his old age Merlin confided his magical secrets to his beloved Viviane, who then betrayed him by imprisoning him in a dungeon, as this painting shows.

IN UNISON
The three witches in Shakespeare's play *Macbeth* – who create evil magic in their cauldron to encourage Macbeth to kill the king and take the Scottish throne – are among literature's best-known sorceresses. This painting by Henry Fuseli (1741–1825) shows them as the ugly "midnight hags" of the bard's imagining.

IMMORTAL MAGICIAN
Merlin lives on in fiction as a good wizard who helps King Arthur fight the forces of evil; here he is played by the actor Nicol Williamson, dressed in an iron skullcap instead of a hooded robe, in the 1981 film *Excalibur*.

EVIL QUEEN
This painting depicts an old English legend about Rosamund, mistress of King Henry II in 1174. The story goes that Henry kept Rosamund hidden in a maze-like house, but the queen, Eleanor, who was thought to be a witch, found her by following a thread; she then poisoned Rosamund.

DRESSED IN RAGS
This tattered costume was worn by one of the three witches in a Royal Shakespeare Company production of *Macbeth* at Stratford, England. In theatrical superstition, just saying "Macbeth" aloud is thought to invite disaster on a production.

Witch ways

The masters of fiction have always been fascinated by stories about witches and innocents, as a means of exploring the battle between good and evil. However, fictional witches are not always portrayed as hags; often they appear as ordinary housewives or glamorous enchantresses.

ULTIMATE EVIL
Truly a Hollywood hag to end all hags – here the actress Anjelica Huston is fearsomely and unrecognizably made up as leader of the evil forces in the 1990 movie *The Witches*.

MIRROR, MIRROR ON THE WALL
In the fairy tale "Snow White and the Seven Dwarfs," the vain and wicked witch-queen asks her magic mirror, "Who is the fairest of them all?" When the reply is "Snow White," the queen decides to kill her young rival with a poisoned apple.

SPINNING WITCH
Here the beautiful young princess is about to fall asleep after pricking her finger on the evil witch's spindle, from the famous fairy tale "Sleeping Beauty" by the 19th-century German writers Jacob and Wilhelm Grimm.

WITCH LADDER
The Brothers Grimm have provided generations of children with many memorable witch stories. In this tale, a jealous witch has imprisoned the lovely Rapunzel in a tower and uses Rapunzel's long hair to climb to the top.

READY FOR BATTLE
This still from the 1963 film *The Raven* shows the actor Boris Karloff (best known for playing Frankenstein's monster in many Hollywood movies) as an evil sorcerer preparing to take on his rival, played in the film by Vincent Price.

WITCH GLAMOUR
In the lighthearted 1942 movie *I Married a Witch*, Veronica Lake starred as a seductive blonde witch (come back to life after being burned in 1692) who is determined to make the hero (played by Fredric March) fall in love with her and desert his fiancée.

WITCH ALERT
Witches are common in folktales all over Europe. Russian stories tell of the witch Baba Yaga, who, as this illustration shows, flies around the dense forests in a mortar and pestle rather than a broomstick.

SKY RIDERS
This drawing by Arthur Rackham (1867–1939) is from the comic-fantasy *Ingoldsby Legends* by "Thomas Ingoldsby" (R. H. Barham, 1788–1845). These witches have enticed a local idler to join their flying frolic.

JOINING FORCES
This still from the 1987 film *The Witches of Eastwick*, from the novel by John Updike, shows three friends (played by Cher, Michelle Pfeiffer, and Susan Sarandon) who have each been seduced and given witch powers by the devil (Jack Nicholson). Here they use their magic to get rid of him.

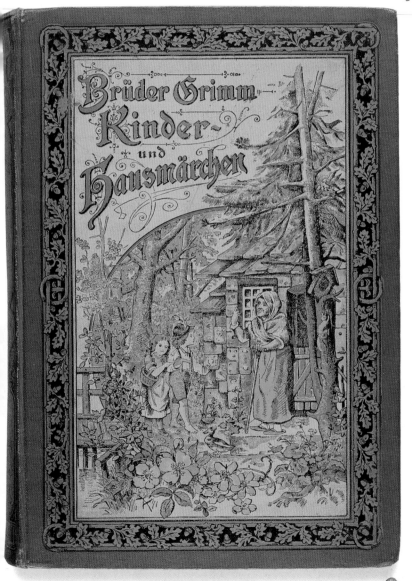

GINGERBREAD HOUSE
One of the Brothers Grimm's scariest inventions was the cannibal witch in "Hansel and Gretel," seen on this front cover of an 1892 collection of their fairy tales. The witch, posing as a friendly old woman, is luring the lost children into her house.

OFF TO SEE THE WIZARD
The classic children's novel *The Wizard of Oz*, by L. Frank Baum (1856–1919), was made into a film in 1939. Here Dorothy (Judy Garland) meets the Wicked Witch of the West.

Magical ancients

THOUSANDS OF YEARS AGO, our ancestors' slow rise from living simple, nomadic lifestyles led to the growth of the great civilizations of the ancient world, including Assyria, Babylon, Egypt, and later, Greece, Persia, and Rome. Previously, for primitive humanity, magic had been concerned with mere *survival* – finding food, avoiding disease, trying to work out the mysteries of nature, and appeasing the gods and spirits. But in the urban civilizations, that early magic-making had evolved into a highly specialised profession with obscure and complex systems of secret beliefs. Although closely bound up with organized religion, these carried a wealth of mysterious traditions to keep the amateurs out. Indeed, many ancient practices, particularly Egyptian, have survived and thrive in magic-making today.

SACRED FLAMES
This gold plaque dating to around 500 B.C. shows a priest-magician of ancient Persia. The Persians worshipped fire, and the priest is carrying a bundle of special twigs, the *barsom*, to feed the ceremonial flames.

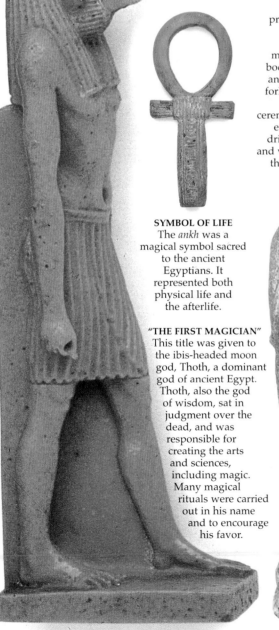

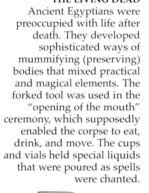

SYMBOL OF LIFE
The *ankh* was a magical symbol sacred to the ancient Egyptians. It represented both physical life and the afterlife.

"THE FIRST MAGICIAN"
This title was given to the ibis-headed moon god, Thoth, a dominant god of ancient Egypt. Thoth, also the god of wisdom, sat in judgment over the dead, and was responsible for creating the arts and sciences, including magic. Many magical rituals were carried out in his name and to encourage his favor.

THE LIVING DEAD
Ancient Egyptians were preoccupied with life after death. They developed sophisticated ways of mummifying (preserving) bodies that mixed practical and magical elements. The forked tool was used in the "opening of the mouth" ceremony, which supposedly enabled the corpse to eat, drink, and move. The cups and vials held special liquids that were poured as spells were chanted.

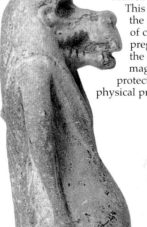

FIERCE PROTECTOR
This statuette represents Taweret, the ancient Egyptian goddess of childbirth, depicted as a pregnant hippopotamus. With the usual tangle of religion and magic, Taweret was believed to protect mothers-to-be against both physical problems and evil sorcery.

FATEFUL MEETING
This engraving portrays one stage in the initiation of an ancient Egyptian sorcerer. During the ceremony, the terrible scythe-carrying figure of Death himself has been conjured up by the master sorcerers to confront the initiate, as a fearsome test of his magical aptitude and nerve.

A HEAVY HEART
Anubis, the jackal-headed god of death, shown here in a detail from an ancient Egyptian papyrus, guides a deceased man into the underworld. On special scales, he "weighs the heart" of the dead man as a measure of the worth of the man's life. If the deceased failed this test, he would be consumed by the reptilian-headed "Devourer of the Dead." The papyrus forms part of the Egyptian *Book of the Dead*, which was the inspiration behind many magical practices.

Magical snake symbol

Cockatrice

Pine cone

POINTED MAGIC
Dating to the first century A.D., this bronze nail decorated with magic symbols is proof of witchery in Roman times. It may have been made for a spell in which an incantation was recited as the nail was slowly hammered into a special wooden surface.

HELPING HAND
This magical bronze hand from ancient Rome was used as a talisman to ward off evil. The pinecone symbolizes the Greek god Dionysus – often linked with witches' wilder rituals – while the serpent with a cockerel's head is the mythical "cockatrice," a monster that could kill with a glance.

WITCH GODDESS
Hecate, the ancient Greek goddess of the underworld, was often shown with three different faces, as in this third century B.C. statue. Seen as a dangerous force, she was the patron of witchcraft and magic, as well as a tormentor of humans, roaming the earth at night with a pack of red-eyed hell hounds.

THE DELPHIC ORACLE
In ancient Greece, people visited a sacred grove at Delphi where a priestess would give magically prophetic, but often mystifying, answers to their questions. This 19th-century illustration shows the priestess writhing in a deep trance.

MAGICAL INCANTATION BOWL
Inscribed with a spell, this bowl was buried under a house in Mesopotamia (modern Iraq), for protection. It dates to the fifth century A.D. and reveals how older pagan beliefs survived the rise of later religions, including Christianity.

Hunt the witch

After the fall of the Roman Empire, Christianity became, in time, the dominant religion of Europe. Yet much of the ancient world's "pagan" traditions, including magic-making, lingered on and thrived among ordinary people. Convinced that such leftover beliefs were inspired by the devil, and determined to stamp them out, the Christian Church launched a merciless and brutal attack on every hint of witchcraft and wizardry throughout Europe. This persecution lasted from the 15th to the 18th century. Hundreds of thousands of helpless suspects suffered torture and execution, often on false charges and faked evidence. Even today, when groups are hounded by a powerful authority, we call it a "witch-hunt."

ONE BRAVE VOICE
A few sympathetic individuals dared to speak out against the witch mania, such as Johann Weyer (1515–88), a German physician. He attacked the brutality and fraudulence of "confessions" extracted through torture, insisting that many so-called witches were harmless innocents, even if deluded.

SATAN'S SERVANTS
To the Church in the Middle Ages, all magic was believed to be the devil's work, and all magic-makers to have sworn allegiance to him. In this 16th-century engraving, two witches, male and female, are shown waiting on a particularly monstrous, enthroned Satan.

DEATH BY FIRE
An illustration in a 1555 newsletter from Derneburg, Germany, shows witches being burned alive at the stake – a widespread form of execution. The artist has added a fanciful image of the devil as a dragon in the sky, claiming the witches' souls as they perish.

PUBLIC HANGING
This woodcut portrays the killing of three witches after a notorious trial in Chelmsford, England, in 1589. Many convictions were based solely on the evidence of very young children, along with the usual torture-induced confessions.

Plate restricted facial and jaw movements

MASK OF FEAR
This crude iron mask was an exotic torture device that was clamped tightly over the face and scalp of a hapless victim, and fastened at the scruff of the neck. Known as a "scold's bridle," it was designed to silence naggers and slanderers as well as suspected witches, and to cause them maximum discomfort and humiliation.

Head brace

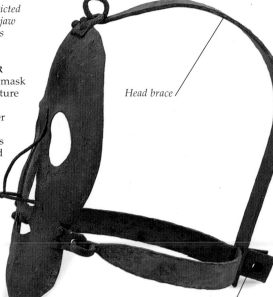

Iron clasp

WITCH'S COLLAR

Testifying to the barbarism of the witch-hunts, this contraption locked around a victim's neck with its savage spikes and held fast with springs. It would then be fixed onto the end of a long pole, and the suspect dragged through the streets – perhaps on the way to a public execution. Townsfolk would typically taunt the unlucky victim.

DEADLY SPIKES

This bronze statuette (after the original) represents a life-size, medieval instrument of torture known as the Black Virgin of Nüremberg. Witches suspected of sorcery were pushed inside the chamber and the spiked door forced shut. Not surprisingly, few survived.

WITCH-FINDER GENERAL

Matthew Hopkins (d.1647), England's most infamous witch-hunter, was said to have hanged more witches in 14 months than all the members of his profession put together had executed in the preceding 160 years. His methods were extremely suspect and his popularity, fortunately, was short-lived.

WITCH SCALES

This iron chair is a replica of one used in Plymouth, England, to test for witches. The accused would be strapped into the device and weighed on a scale against the two huge volumes of the Plymouth Bible. Weighing less than that Holy Book (as many would) proved the victim's guilt.

TRIAL BY DUCKING

Witches, went the belief, cannot drown, since clean water rejects them. So the accused would be bound and tested by "swimming," as shown in this woodcut. If she sank she was innocent, but if she floated, she was clearly a witch.

OPEN WIDE

Another extreme device used by the witch-hunters was this simple screw mechanism used to force a victim's mouth wide open. Sometimes, gallons of water or other liquids would be poured down the tormented victim's throat in order to force a confession.

The Salem trials

THE WITCH-HUNTING FRENZY that plagued Europe reached as far as the American colonies, where perhaps the worst outbreak took place in 1692 in Salem, Massachusetts. The colonists were tense and troubled even beforehand, because of hostility from the French to the north as well as frequent Indian raids. The panic started when a group of girls began dabbling, for thrills, in folk magic – at a time when many people were convinced of the menace of "Satanic" witchcraft. The girls showed signs (perhaps faked) of strange illnesses, then began accusing other villagers (of all social levels) of being witches. Salem was soon gripped by terror – and what may have begun merely as an attention-seeking prank ended with 141 arrests and 20 executions (tragically, only those who denied being witches were killed).

IN THE NAME OF THE LAW
As the hysteria spread, the girls from Salem were called upon to identify witches in neighboring communities. This illustration shows the arrest of an elderly, lame woman; such people were vulnerable and made easy targets.

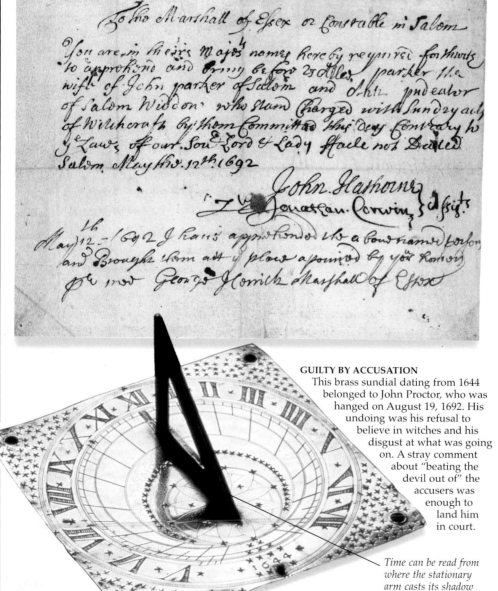

SURVIVING DOCUMENT
This is the actual warrant for the arrest of Ann Pudeator, who was convicted by the court and hanged as a witch on September 22, 1692. The miscarriage of justice at Salem was inexcusable and shocking – especially the "supernatural" evidence offered by the girls. The jurors at the trials officially apologized for their part in the fiasco four years later.

GUILTY BY ACCUSATION
This brass sundial dating from 1644 belonged to John Proctor, who was hanged on August 19, 1692. His undoing was his refusal to believe in witches and his disgust at what was going on. A stray comment about "beating the devil out of" the accusers was enough to land him in court.

Time can be read from where the stationary arm casts its shadow

"SHE'S A WITCH!"
This illustration shows a typical court scene during the Salem trials. The accused would stand before the group of girls, who would promptly become hysterical and go into violent fits as if in agony, an act that was evidently quite convincing. They claimed that the accused were "spectrally" appearing before them and summoning demons to torment them.

CLASSIC DRAMA
The story of the events and panic at Salem was dramatized by the playwright Arthur Miller in *The Crucible*, written in 1953. The play has been popular ever since; this scene is from a 1990 production at the National Theatre in London.

Different kinds of stitch show embroiderer's skill

SOLEMN REMINDER
This photograph dating from 1850 shows the monument erected in memory of Rebecca Nurse, a well-respected member of the Salem community who had been born in 1621 in Yarmouth, England. She was accused, condemned to death, and hanged as a witch on July 19, 1692. She was bedridden at the time of accusation and she protested her innocence to the end.

INTRICATE WORK
This sampler (a piece of embroidery demonstrating the needleworker's skill) was made in 1665 by Mary Hollingsworth of Salem. She later married Philip English, who was one of the many local people who were accused of witchcraft and of willfully trying to hurt the hysterical girls by devilish means. Fortunately, he was not convicted.

Magical rites and tools

FICTIONAL MAGICIANS often seem able to work powerful magic with no more than a word, the flick of a pointed finger, the wave of a wand. But in existing magical traditions there is usually more to it than that. Much of the work of witches and wizards is *ritual magic*, where power is "gathered" and "directed" through a rite or ceremony – short and simple for small acts of magic, long and complex for more ambitious purposes. Most rituals involve a combination of elements, including the recitation of special words or sounds, chants, and choreographed movements. They also require the wielding of many different implements and instruments (each practitioner adopts his or her own), which are sometimes strange but often quite ordinary.

BONE HUNTING
A witch seeking human remains in a graveyard (from an old engraving). Human bones, skulls especially, were highly valued by magic-makers: their eerie connection with death made them potent ritual objects, worth committing the crime of grave robbery to collect.

SORCERER'S STAFF
This iron staff, with its base shaped like a bear's paw, was carried by a tribal shaman in Siberia. While in a deep trance, the shaman used the staff for summoning "nature spirits" to help him work magic in healing and other rituals.

THREE BAGS FULL
The "occult" darkness of a black sheep's fleece made it useful in working magic. It was believed a ball of wool, left in the room a person slept in, would absorb their breath and so could later be used as the main ingredient in a spell to bewitch them.

WAVING WANDS
Two elegant "magic wands" – one of ivory, one of ebony – owned by practicing, well-to-do witches in 1890s London. They were probably used for theatrical effect and ceremonial gestures, or for symbolic, "purifying" beatings.

ANCIENT POWER
A precursor of the *athame* used in modern magic (p. 59), this ivory ceremonial knife is from ancient Egypt. The engraved images of animals and mythical creatures were thought to enhance its power. A wizard would wield the knife rituals or to work a spell – perhaps using it to draw an invisible line of protective magic around a person or a place.

EERIE WIND INSTRUMENT
A horn made from a human thigh bone, used by a Mashona witch doctor in Zimbabwe. It would be blown (like similar instruments from Tibet and elsewhere) to call the spirits of the dead to magic-making ceremonies.

HEALING TOOL
Believing that many illnesses resulted from the "loss of the soul" (perhaps caused by evil magic), shamans of the Tsimshian people of the northwest coast of North America would heal the sick by retrieving their souls with "soul-catchers" like this one. It is in the shape of two sea-lion heads and is carved from elk bone, with an abalone shell inlay.

MAGIC BACKBONE
Notable for its unusually humanlike appearance, this ox's vertebra was painted with the face of a supernatural being. Once the property of a witch in Somerset, England, it may have been used to reinforce her powers in rituals and spell-casting – as if it were her "familiar" spirit (p. 38).

RITUAL RHYTHM
This drum was also used by a Mashona witch-doctor. Like the horn (above), drums were combined with dancing, incantation, and general noise to summon good spirits, drive evil ones away, and put all present into a semi-hypnotic, trancelike state.

SHAMAN IN ACTION
Blindfolded and guided by her intuition, this Thai shaman conducts a ritual in front of a group of mesmerized onlookers in Bangkok. Performing adhoc in the open air, she has carried all her equipment with her. This includes ritual bowls, knives, and a wand, as well as incense, fruit, and candles.

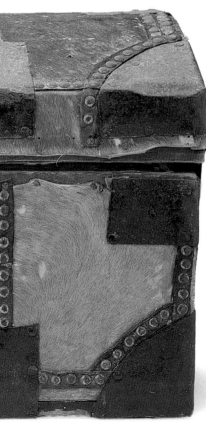

WITCH BOTTLES
Filled with colored essences, these bottles once belonged to an English witch. Some witches used such bottles to store potions; others used them simply for effect, impressing their clients with the bottles' alleged mysterious powers.

SECRET STORAGE
This old trunk belonged to a 19th-century witch living in Birmingham, England. Most magic-makers had a special container of some sort – often called a "trash-box" – for magical tools that had to be kept safe and secret from prying eyes.

Amulets, charms, talismans

THE PRACTICE OF carrying special objects that are believed to possess magical power has existed since early times all over the world. Even today someone might carry a rabbit's foot or a four-leaf clover as a "lucky charm." Such magical objects are properly known as *amulets* and *talismans* – amulets ward off evil (including the effects of evil sorcery) and ill luck, while talismans attract good fortune and happiness. They can be quite ordinary things, like stones, herbs, shells, or parts of animals, which are thought to be imbued with "natural magic." Alternatively, they can be purpose-made (often inexpensively), and inscribed or "injected" with power by professional magic-makers – a good source of income in superstitious areas. Most commonly, amulets and talismans are designed to be worn as jewelry, in the form of pendants or necklaces.

WITCH STONES
Stones with holes in them, like many other unusual naturally occurring objects, were thought to have magical properties.

HELPING HAND
A brass representation of the hand of Fatima, daughter of Mohammed – a popular talisman all over the Arab world.

MAGIC SCRIPT
This shell amulet from the Near East bears an inscription in Arabic. The purity of its color adds to its magical power to drive away evil.

GLITTERING CHARM
A golden, 19th-century Arab amulet depicting the sun and the moon and edged with sparkling stones – to counteract dark magic.

Engraved crescent moon

SACRED IMAGE
Magic and religion meet in this amulet necklace from India, which bears the image of the kindly elephant-god, Ganesha.

Ganesha painted on amulet box

HEARTFELT WORDS
This paper square from the Middle East bears a "talismanic" inscription in Arabic. It would have been folded and carried in the triangular pouch (right) at all times.

ON THE MIND
The cloth amulet pouch would have been worn next to the skin, so the wearer would feel it as he walked and be constantly reminded of its magical contents.

CONTENTED CATTLE
In Ethiopia, fertility amulets like this are still worn by the Galla people to ensure the health and successful breeding of their herds – proving the survival of pagan traditions despite the predominance of Christianity.

Charms made of horn

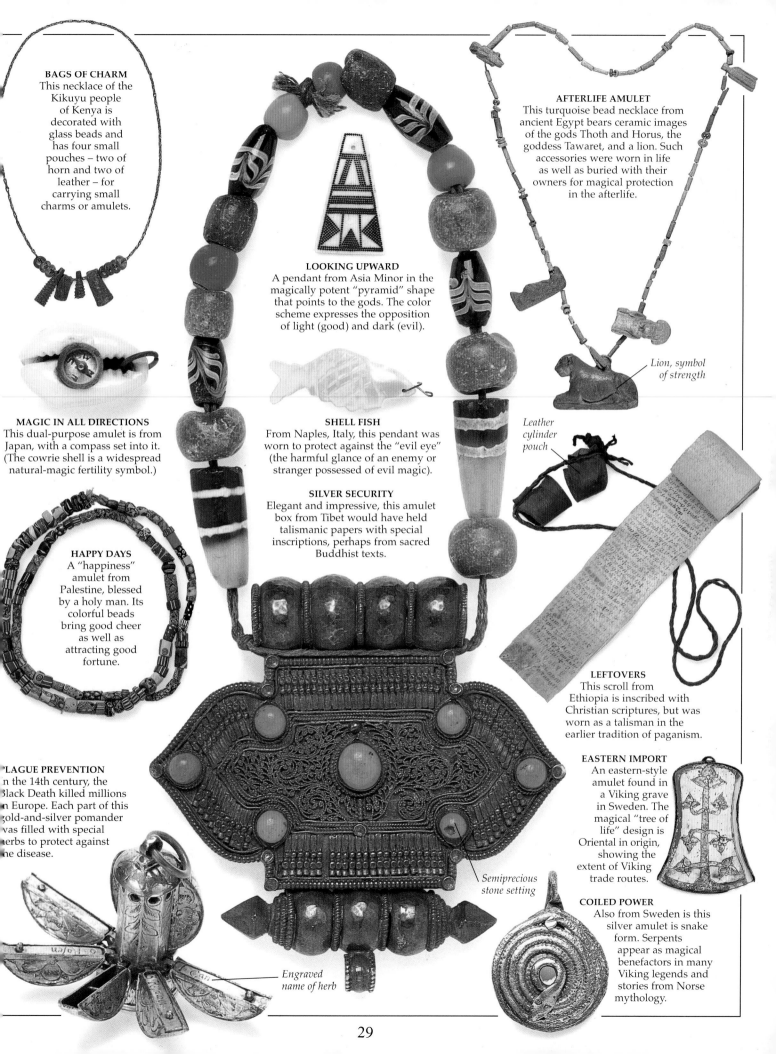

BAGS OF CHARM
This necklace of the Kikuyu people of Kenya is decorated with glass beads and has four small pouches – two of horn and two of leather – for carrying small charms or amulets.

MAGIC IN ALL DIRECTIONS
This dual-purpose amulet is from Japan, with a compass set into it. (The cowrie shell is a widespread natural-magic fertility symbol.)

HAPPY DAYS
A "happiness" amulet from Palestine, blessed by a holy man. Its colorful beads bring good cheer as well as attracting good fortune.

PLAGUE PREVENTION
In the 14th century, the Black Death killed millions in Europe. Each part of this gold-and-silver pomander was filled with special herbs to protect against the disease.

LOOKING UPWARD
A pendant from Asia Minor in the magically potent "pyramid" shape that points to the gods. The color scheme expresses the opposition of light (good) and dark (evil).

SHELL FISH
From Naples, Italy, this pendant was worn to protect against the "evil eye" (the harmful glance of an enemy or stranger possessed of evil magic).

SILVER SECURITY
Elegant and impressive, this amulet box from Tibet would have held talismanic papers with special inscriptions, perhaps from sacred Buddhist texts.

Engraved name of herb

AFTERLIFE AMULET
This turquoise bead necklace from ancient Egypt bears ceramic images of the gods Thoth and Horus, the goddess Tawaret, and a lion. Such accessories were worn in life as well as buried with their owners for magical protection in the afterlife.

Lion, symbol of strength

Leather cylinder pouch

LEFTOVERS
This scroll from Ethiopia is inscribed with Christian scriptures, but was worn as a talisman in the earlier tradition of paganism.

EASTERN IMPORT
An eastern-style amulet found in a Viking grave in Sweden. The magical "tree of life" design is Oriental in origin, showing the extent of Viking trade routes.

Semiprecious stone setting

COILED POWER
Also from Sweden is this silver amulet is snake form. Serpents appear as magical benefactors in many Viking legends and stories from Norse mythology.

Under cover

When not hanging around someone's neck, talismans and amulets might be sewn into the lining of a garment or carried in a pocket or pouch of leather or silk, for secrecy as well as safekeeping. Touching the object in a troubled moment would reassure its owner and reinforce his or her sense of its magic power. In fact, much of an amulet's effectiveness may come simply from the wearer's faith in it, an often subconscious *certainty* that it works.

FESTIVAL CHARM
Mexico's "Day of the Dead" celebrations honor ancestors and seek their good will. Token skulls and bones are carried as powerful good-luck charms.

ROYAL TOUCH
English gold coins from the 1700s, when a king's touch was thought to have healing power. These "touchpieces", fingered by the king, were given to the sick.

ANCIENT STONE
This holed roundel of neolithic sandstone from Devon, England, was prized as an amulet against ill luck and the spells of evil witches, including curdling the milk.

LIFE PRESERVER
An "astragal" (sheep's ankle bone) was used since early times for gambling, but was also carried by English fishermen as an amulet against drowning in high seas.

RUSTIC CHARM
A plain horseshoe was considered lucky because cold iron was thought to keep evil witches away. Its shape is similar to the crescent moon, a traditional magical symbol.

SECRET SYMBOL
Drawn on a 14th-century Egyptian scroll, this cryptic, talismanic magic symbol was used to implant power into charms and amulets.

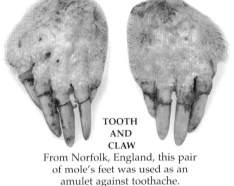

TOOTH AND CLAW
From Norfolk, England, this pair of mole's feet was used as an amulet against toothache.

PRAYER DISK
Another example of sacred writing used for talismanic protection is this metal disk charm bearing the initial letters of the words of a Jewish prayer.

FEARSOME JAWS
This amulet in the form of an alligator head, from Motu-Motu, New Guinea was worn to protect the wearer against the creatures, or to bring success to those who hunted them.

"EYE OF RA"
This ceramic amulet bears the powerful all-seeing "eye" of the ancient Egyptian sun god, Ra.

MARITIME MAGIC
Originating from southern Italy, this dried seahorse was carried to ward off evil sorcery. The creature was traditionally considered magical simply because of its beauty and strangeness.

Charm pouch

BENIGN DEITY
This stone rubbing from China, used as a talisman, depicts a Taoist god. Many Taoist images had a magical purpose – mainly to ensure long life and good fortune.

STARING EYES
The "lids" of mollusk shells, uncannily resembling eyeballs, are widely used as amulets in southern Italy (where they are called the "Eyes of St. Lucia") to ward off evil influences.

ANTI-SERPENT PROTECTION
The spiky seed of a *Martynia*, or "unicorn" plant, used in India as an amulet against venomous snake bites.

WITCH WOOD
Formed from the natural knothole of a tree branch, this amulet from rural England may once have been used by a witch in her magic-making.

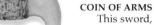

ARCTIC AMULET
This token, carved from bone in the form of a strange animal, was fixed to the clothes of a shaman in Alaska, for protection.

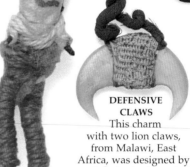

DEFENSIVE CLAWS
This charm with two lion claws, from Malawi, East Africa, was designed by a witch doctor to protect against lions and to draw their strength to the wearer.

COIN OF ARMS
This sword, made of holed coins strung together on red cord, was made as a protective amulet for a new baby boy in China, to drive away evil spirits.

HELPFUL SPRITE
This "trouble doll" amulet, made of colored twine, is from Guatemala and was thought to take on a person's worries.

BE HAPPY
A "happiness" charm from Turkey; the central flower design and the seven diamante "stars" represent peace, prosperity, good luck, and a happy home.

HANDS OFF
This fist-shaped amulet from Italy, the *mano fica*, is an amulet to "hold off" the evil eye and other sinister magic.

Staring eyes

Red ocher paint

FEARFUL FACE
A pumice-stone amulet from Murray Island in Torres Strait off Australia, carved and painted in a grotesque manner to frighten away evil spirits.

AMULET ARMOR
This protective battle gown was used by the Ashantí people of Africa. Each pouch contains written charm quotations from the Korán, the sacred scriptures of Islam.

Bewitched!

EVIL IMAGE
To aim a curse or malicious spell at a person, a witch has dressed this clay "hex doll" to resemble that person. In more recent times, witches might also have pinned a snapshot of the person to the doll's clothing.

W HEN WITCHES OR WIZARDS are "casting spells," they are working very specific acts of magic. A spell is almost always a kind of formula, which might use incantations (recited words or chants), various potions, images, and implements. These elements are designed to gather magical power and direct it toward a special purpose – to "bewitch" someone or something (for good or ill), to effect some kind of change, or to inject magic into healing remedies or objects. The formulas (often recorded in special spell books) can be as simple as a few words muttered over a herbal brew; but the most impressive spells are worked by means of the elaborate and mysterious ceremonies of "ritual magic."

FEARFUL INJECTION
This medieval woodcut shows a witch preparing to shoot a twig into a man's foot – in order to "infect" him with evil. However, most real witches used plants and herbs for *healing* purposes.

PAPER SPELL
This is a simple spell prescribed by magic-workers in China. The desired aims of the spell are first written within the circle and mystic hand. Then the "charmed" paper is burned and the ashes stirred into water and drunk.

AFRICAN LOVE ARROWS
This miniature bow and arrows are used by the San people of southern Africa to work love magic. A man shoots an arrow – harmlessly, symbolically – at a woman he wants to fall in love with him, just like Cupid's arrows in European mythology.

GRUESOME FINGERS
A favorite object of evil witchcraft in the past was the "hand of glory," cut from a corpse and dried. Used either as a candleholder or set alight itself, the hand was believed to have the power to stupefy people (it was especially popular with burglars!) and to reinforce spells.

HAPPY COUPLE
These Native American wooden dolls have nothing to do with hexes (malicious spells). Representing a husband and wife, they contain "love medicines" (ointments and herbs) in a cavity in the front of each, and were tied face to face – to symbolize and protect the permanence of a marriage.

HORSE GUARDS

This thigh bone of a cow on a chain, from Devon, England, was "magicked" by a kindly local witch and hung by a stable door to protect the horses inside from thieves and from wicked witches who might steal them for "night-riding."

HEAVY CURSE

A Roman lead tablet inscribed with a curse aimed at robbers. In recent times, lead (stolen from a church roof) has remained the choice for carrying curses.

ON THE NAIL

Iron nails like these, infused with magic power, are sometimes irreverently called "Jesus nails," because they were intended to be hammered slowly into sacred ground (like a churchyard) at night, to reinforce a spell or incantation.

WHATKNOT

Making a "witch knot" was a well-known way to gather and "tie up" magic energy. This one, from the south of England, is a lover's knot – made with a flexible twig and knotted while the name of the one whose love was sought was sung out loud.

Henbane

Deadly nightshade

PLANT POWER

This old woodcut shows the legendary mandrake plant in personified form. The root of the plant was said to be the most potent herb of all; it could work mighty spells, and could kill the one who dared to uproot it (hence, dogs were used to perform this task).

WHAT'S ON THE MENU?

This 19th-century lithograph depicts a typical witch at work, sitting on her stool and studying a recipe from her spell-book. Her feline "familiar" (pp. 38–39) is at her side, and the ingredients for the magic she is boiling up in her cauldron are within easy reach.

Wolfsbane

HARD POUND

No witch has ever been without a mortar (left) and pestle (below) for grinding up ingredients for spells. These once belonged to a working witch in Cornwall, England.

Hemlock

LIFT-OFF CREAM

Witches were thought to gain the power to fly from smearing on a special ointment made with the plants pictured here, among other ingredients. All four are poisonous, and substances made from them may well have produced hallucinations – of flying, for example.

Magical ingredients

MAGIC-MAKERS AROUND the world have always been adept at what might be called "magical cookery" – the concocting of potions, ointments, and infusions – as well as the preparation of all sorts of dry ingredients for sewing into "charm bags" or for working simple spells. On the local level, any village or tribal magic-maker would have had, and in many cases still does have, an encyclopedic knowledge of plants, herbs, and natural substances, and of "recipes" for magic brews of all sorts. Of course, good witches know all about folk medicines and beneficial mixtures, while wicked witches specialize in poisons and vile mixtures suited to their evil ends.

SEEDS OF LOVE
In this traditional Chinese love potion, a handful of coriander seeds are crushed and stirred into a glass of white wine while the person chants: "Warm seed, love run strong; warm heart, let us never part." The lovers drink the wine, and their love is assured.

Lavender

Green ribbon

Wooden skewer

Sprig of fresh mint

ENCHANTED WORDS
This enduring spell shows how herbalism is used to write successful letters (for love or business). A sheet of stationery is rubbed all over with fragrant lavender, and the letter is written in a crimson ink called "dove's blood" to ensure that the correspondent's wishes are granted.

SPELL APPLE
A simple "banishing" spell prescribed by a modern witch uses an apple cut in half sideways. One half is rubbed with mint while the bad habit or problem to be banished is repeated aloud. The halves are then rejoined with a skewer, tied with ribbon, and buried. As the apple rots, the problem will depart.

Ink bottle

WHAT'S HIS NAME?
This folk magic required a girl to write the alphabet on squares of cardboard, which were left, facedown, in water overnight. The letters turned faceup in the morning were thought to be the initials of the one she was to marry.

FRIENDS FOREVER
To ensure an enduring friendship, some cloves are sewn up into two little bags, each one carried at all times by the friends concerned

BUDDING AFFECTION
A long-lived spell for a person wanting to fall in love is to put a bag of rosebuds (roses have always been magically linked to love) in the water each time he or she takes a bath.

Sachet bag is made of muslin

Sage

Rosemary

Thyme

AROMATIC MAGIC
This herbal spell is an old favorite to attract love: a sachet bag of sage, rosemary, and thyme is kept in a drawer or under a pillow, or even worn next to the skin. The bag must be moistened every seven days with seven drops of bergamot oil to be truly effective in delivering your heart's desire.

Honeysuckle

String has 31 knots tied in it, symbolizing the days of the month

One bill for each month of the year

Orris root

SWEET DREAMS
For a magic pillow, red rose petals, honeysuckle flowers, powdered orris root, allspice, and a lock of the spellmaker's own hair are placed together and sewn up in muslin. The bag should then be moistened liberally with oil of pine. Asleep on this, your beloved should dream only of you!

Allspice

Oil of pine

Box must have a secure lid

PROFITABLE THYME
This spell was used to make money, literally. Twelve bits of banknote-sized paper are placed in a box, with thyme sprinkled between each piece. The box is then tied with green string in 31 knots and buried seven inches deep. It is believed that if it is dug up one year later, it will contain real money.

Powdered orris root

Rosemary

LOVE BATH
This watery love magic is a potion to add to a bath, to make a person irresistible. The mixture consists of rosemary and thyme, steeped in boiling water (preferably in an earthenware jug), with powdered orris root and lovage root added later. The mixture should be strained and stirred before being poured into the bathwater.

Thyme

Lovage root

ABSORBENT ONIONS
Banish "negative" energy by placing an onion quarter in each corner of your room overnight. Next day, wearing rubber gloves, chop them up and bury them. Do this daily for three to seven days.

Divining arts

SINCE EARLIEST TIMES, one of the specialities of professional magic-makers has been to divine, or discover, unknown things, usually by supposed supernatural forces. Divining could bring an answer to a client's question or reveal a proper course of action. Predicting the future and peering into the past have also been part of their repertoire. (And they still are, although modern fortune-tellers might say that their work is not magic but an art or science.) An amazing range of techniques has been used for these prophetic glimpses: sundry objects scattered at random (bones on the ground, tea leaves in a cup); information gleaned from the stars or the lines on a person's hand; readings taken from dreams, crystals, animal entrails, or packs of cards; or merely prophesying while in a trance.

IN THE CRACKS
Royal "oracle bones" used during the Shang period in China (c.1550–c.1050 B.C.). After the king's question was inscribed on the bone, it would be heated. The cracks that formed would reveal the answer, which would then be recorded on the bone.

Text reveals the date, inquirer's name, the question, and the interpretation

OLD HAND
A Tibetan palmist tells the fortune of a Nepalese trader in 1951 – just as fortunes have been told all over Asia, and all over the world, for centuries.

PROPHETIC VISION
A shaman in Lapland lying in a trance induced by a magical ceremony, with a ritual drum placed on his back. In the trance, the shaman would see, and reveal, visions of the future or answers to questions and mysteries.

Marriage Lines
Heart Line
Head Line
Life Line
Line of Mercury
Line of Apollo
Line of Saturn
Travel Lines

In palmistry, the raised area below the thumb is called the "mount of Venus"

The Hand

PIN POWER
A simple means of divination used by a witch in Devon, England. As the candle burned, the witch read answers to her clients' questions according to how and where the pins fell into the tin holder.

ON LINE
This china model shows the major "lines of destiny" studied in palmistry – the heart line, running horizontally below the fingers, the head line, just under it, and the life line, curving down toward the wrist.

WATER FINDERS
A forked birch twig used in dowsing, sometimes called "water divining," to locate underground water (or even oil and buried treasure). Dowsers are even used by many modern oil and water companies.

Spiked ends have been smoothed and polished

MAGIC POINTER
A divining staff from Mozambique, Africa, mainly used to identify individuals responsible for some evildoing. The witch doctor moved the staff around at random among the gathered villagers until it seemed to point at the guilty party.

INNER ORGANS
A clay model of a sheep's liver with markings in cuneiform script (perhaps used to instruct apprentice diviners) from 18th-century B.C. Mesopotamia. Similar forms of fortune-telling, including reading the entrails of sacrificed animals, have been around since the start of recorded history.

Crocodile shape

Peg

MYSTIC CARDS
Two of the 78 cards of the Tarot pack, which is so old that its origins are unknown. The complex lore involved in reading the symbolism of the cards and their layouts requires years of study.

CROCODILE TRUTH
This wooden palette was used for divination among the Kuba people of Zaire. First a witch doctor would put oil on its smooth back, then rub it with the peg while calling out likely answers to a villager's questions. When the peg seemed to stick, the answer being spoken at that moment was the right one.

CRYSTAL CLEAR
A crystal ball (made by Baccarat, a leading glass manufacturer) on a stand representing Atlas, the Titan of Greek mythology. The best crystals for "scrying" (crystal-gazing) are of semi-precious stone, like beryl. While in a trance, diviners use the crystal ball to seek visions.

THROWING BONES
A diviner in South Africa, with a client, scattering small objects on a mat and reading the future, or answers to questions, in their random patterns. Today, shells and coins are often used instead of the traditional bones.

Animal magic

SHAPE-SHIFTERS
Witches were commonly believed to be able to change shape into animal forms. In this 15th-century woodcut, three witches flying to a sabbath, or gathering, have disguised themselves as domestic creatures – a donkey, a cockerel, and a dog.

Mᴀɢɪᴄ ʜᴀs ᴍᴀᴅᴇ ᴍᴜᴄʜ use of animals, not always pleasantly. In different parts of the world, anything from one chicken to a herd of cattle has been slaughtered as a sacrifice to please the spirits or to reinforce a ritual. Magic-makers have concocted potions using bits of animals and blood, and fashioned ritual costumes with hides, furs, and horns. They have read omens in the flight of birds and foretold the future in animal entrails. Many witches have also kept an animal as a magical pet – the witch's "familiar," an imp in animal form, which lends the witch its supernatural powers. So for witch-hunters of the past, having mice or a pet cat, or even a large spider's web in a corner of your parlor, was proof of witchcraft and consorting with demons.

MAGICAL PROPERTIES
This stuffed, two-headed lamb once belonged to a village witch in Somerset, England. Such "freaks of nature," deemed to be magically potent due to their strangeness and rarity, have always been highly prized and jealously guarded by magic-makers.

DEVILISH REVELRY
In this detail of a comic painting, *A Diablerie*, by Cornelius Saftleven (1607–81), lesser demons are depicted in animal form. But instead of the supposed debauchery of Satan-worshipping rites, these mischievous spirits are equipped for tamer pursuits like tennis and backgammon.

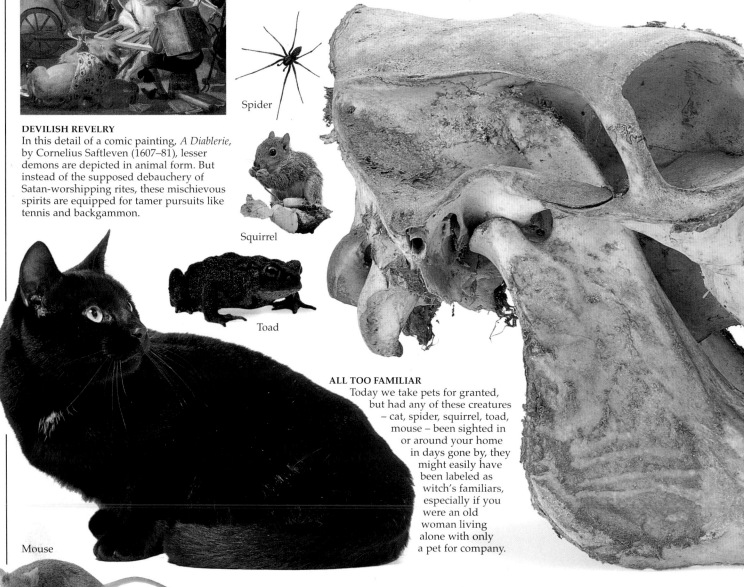

Spider

Squirrel

Toad

Mouse

ALL TOO FAMILIAR
Today we take pets for granted, but had any of these creatures – cat, spider, squirrel, toad, mouse – been sighted in or around your home in days gone by, they might easily have been labeled as witch's familiars, especially if you were an old woman living alone with only a pet for company.

SLITHERING SERPENTS
Snakes play a prominent role in magic-making the world over, most likely because of man's age-old dread of them. Often perceived to be gods or devils in disguise, live snakes are used in rituals, and the skins, fangs, and venom of poisonous snakes are common ingredients in spells and potions.

SORCERER'S BONDING RING
Treasured by a witch doctor of the Mashona tribe of southern Zimbabwe, this magic tool was made from the tusks of a wild boar. The tusks have grown together to form a perfect circle, which is very rare, giving it magical power. The ring was probably used in the swearing of oaths; a person would put his arm through the ring while making his pledge (which he would never dare to break).

WITCHES INCOGNITO
In Africa, many believe that sorcerers can cloak themselves in the form of scary animals like leopards and hyenas, so they can move around and gather in the bush secretly, unrecognized. In rural areas of Europe, one belief was that witches changed into hares.

Hare

Leopard

Hyena

NIGHT FLIGHTS
In many parts of the world, witches and sorcerers were thought to prefer winged shapes for their nocturnal adventures. Folklore adds that they usually changed into dark and spooky-looking birds like crows, ravens, and owls. Bats were also a favorite.

Crow

Eagle owl

OX SKULL
On the advice of a local witch, perhaps after a run of bad luck or illness in his herd, this ox skull was used by a farmer in England as an "appeasement" symbol. Daily he would respectfully greet the skull, which was positioned prominently in his home or barn – to keep the nature spirits happy and his cattle contented.

GRISLY SOUVENIR
This sheep's heart studded with nails was discovered in a cemetery in the Montmartre quarter of Paris. Clearly it had been used as a form of animal sacrifice in some clandestine but no doubt gruesome spell or rite of modern magic.

African sorcery

As AFRICA IS A VAST continent of varied cultures and peoples, so African witch doctors come in many guises, all with their own ways of casting spells, reading the future, healing, divining, and so on. But their societies can also have some things in common. Art, for example, is central to most African cultures, whether it is the visual arts of stylized carvings and masks or the ceremonial arts of music and dance. And where art exists in Africa, there is magic. Carvings may be "fetishes," objects that are believed to contain spirits and prized as amulets and talismans (pp. 28–31) imbued with magic; masks often represent supernatural spirits or ancestors. Ceremonies may be ritual magic, casting spells or appealing to unseen powers for help and guidance.

RITE AND PROPER
This village witch doctor from Cameroon, West Africa, is typical of tribal magic-makers. The bells on his ankles and gourd rattles on his staff are to call spirits to his rituals.

NAILING ILLNESS
Depending on the accompanying ritual, wooden figures like this one from Central Africa were used either as "hex dolls" for bad magic, where the nails are meant to cause illness in a victim, or for healing magic, where the nails are intended to drive out disease from a sick person.

Ebony carved head

Tube made of bone

Hole for speaking and blowing into

Mirror is a typical feature of nail fetishes

Hidden cavity for magic plants or ointments

DUAL PURPOSE
This miniature carved fetish figure from the Ogowe River region in Zaïre was used to confer protection and good health on a home or person. The back of its head is removable and the cavity inside is used to hold a witch doctor's herbs and other substances for magical use.

SORCERERS' CALLING
This curious instrument, called a "voice disguiser," was used by a witch doctor in Nigeria to summon and communicate with the spirits of the dead.

Decorative seeds pressed into resin base

Etched lines reflect local custom of facial scarring

IN THE POT
This carving is from West Africa. The chicken-shaped container was used by a shaman for storing palm kernels, which were used in a simple method of divining the causes of illness. The woman may represent Odobua Yoruba, mother of the gods, lending her power to the magic-maker.

Male figure represents Eshu, another Yoruba god

SORCEROUS HORNS
This antelope skull from Ghana was preserved, decorated, and mounted by a witch doctor as a special fetish, perhaps for use in spell-making. The "nature spirit" of the animal is believed to bring its own power to the magic. Alternatively, it may have been used as a talisman.

PLEASING THE WITCHES
This carved helmet mask belongs to the "Gelede" society of the Yoruba people of Nigeria – a society or club that acts to protect against witchcraft. The mask is worn with an elaborate costume in a ritual dance intended to subdue and amuse the witches of the local community, and to discourage them from practicing evil sorcery.

Decorative eyes give magical "sight" to the antelope spirit

ANCESTRAL VOICES
These festive dancers in Benin, West Africa, are dressed up as "resurrected ancestors" for a pageant to ensure the ancestors' blessing on the community.

Enduring traditions

From the 15th century onward, when Africa was first being explored by Europeans, magic-making was encountered everywhere. These old ways – shamanic healing and protection, as well as more menacing practices – continue to thrive alongside, and have often mingled with, non-native faiths including Christianity and, in North and East Africa, Islam.

SNAKE REPELLENTS
These magical iron serpent symbols were given by a Mashona witch doctor of Zimbabwe to a local villager. They are "banishing" tools used to keep evil influences and poisonous snakes from entering his house.

MAGIC CATCHER
This hooked tool was held by a Mashona shaman and "drawn" toward him with a pulling action to invite and direct positive energy toward his magical designs.

SPIKY CURE
This iron spike driven through a nut was used as a simple healing magic by a Mashona witch doctor. It symbolized the "driving out" of pain from the head, or perhaps an internal organ.

LIVESTOCK SAFETY
This simple effigy of an animal, perhaps a cow or goat, is made of crude rubber. Its hind legs are bound with raffia (palm fibre) to magically keep the farmer's herd from wandering off or being stolen.

TAIL OF ENCHANTMENT
African witch doctors often strengthen their spells by using parts of animals as magical fetishes (p. 40), like this elephant's tail from Sette Cama in the Gabon, West Africa.

Hippopotamus tooth

Twig and string bundle

Spoon

Spatula

Shell bundle

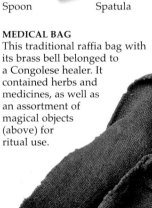

MEDICAL BAG
This traditional raffia bag with its brass bell belonged to a Congolese healer. It contained herbs and medicines, as well as an assortment of magical objects (above) for ritual use.

BEDSIDE MANNER
This shaman of the Ng'anga people of Zambia is engaged in his traditional healing practice. With headdress and rattle, and magical twigs placed on the patient's abdomen, he chants a spell to cast out the ailment.

RED FOR DANGER
The red powder in this English-made jar comes from Malawi in East Africa. The powder, called "mwaboi," has long been used by local witch doctors as a magical poison to identify witches, who were supposed to be abnormally affected by it.

SPELL-BINDER
This bizarre, antique carved wooden bust of a woman, draped in a head scarf and shoulder cloth, belonged to a magic-maker of the Mende people in Sierra Leone. Judging from its somewhat eerie appearance and realistic adornment, it was probably thought to contain a witch's power for use in casting spells, and perhaps curses.

Earrings and cowrie shell necklace add to realistic effect

Carving is crude, proving that its primary purpose was not decorative

TRIAL BY ORDEAL
In Africa as in Europe, brutal tests have often been used to expose suspected witches. These poisonous seeds, called "ordeal beans," were fed to suspects in Nigeria; if the victims vomited, they were innocent – if they died, this proved their guilt.

CHARMING BITS AND PIECES
These cotton-bound pouches found with the Mende witch effigy (left) contain small charms and fetish objects. Other accessories found with the figure included spearheads and a human arm bone.

SORCERERS' APPRENTICES
These would-be witch doctors in Lome, Togo, are wearing white robes to show their status as witchcraft initiates. They meet together in a local *kapame*, or secret society, to perform magical ceremonies and receive instruction from their seniors.

Native American magic

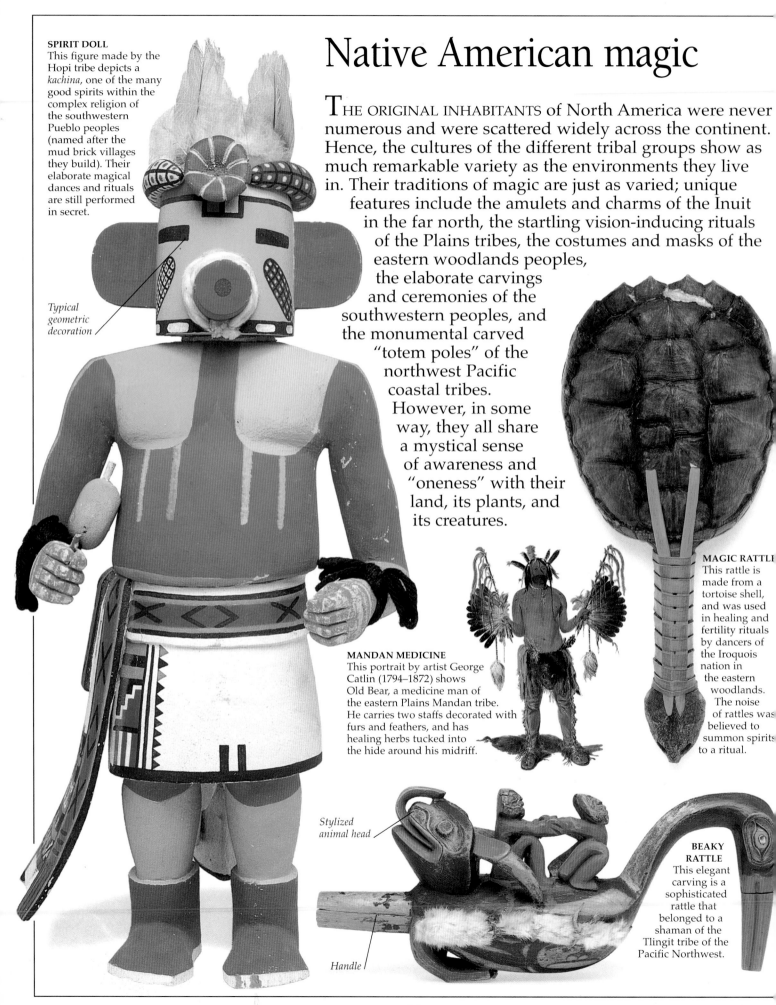

SPIRIT DOLL
This figure made by the Hopi tribe depicts a *kachina*, one of the many good spirits within the complex religion of the southwestern Pueblo peoples (named after the mud brick villages they build). Their elaborate magical dances and rituals are still performed in secret.

Typical geometric decoration

THE ORIGINAL INHABITANTS of North America were never numerous and were scattered widely across the continent. Hence, the cultures of the different tribal groups show as much remarkable variety as the environments they live in. Their traditions of magic are just as varied; unique features include the amulets and charms of the Inuit in the far north, the startling vision-inducing rituals of the Plains tribes, the costumes and masks of the eastern woodlands peoples, the elaborate carvings and ceremonies of the southwestern peoples, and the monumental carved "totem poles" of the northwest Pacific coastal tribes. However, in some way, they all share a mystical sense of awareness and "oneness" with their land, its plants, and its creatures.

MAGIC RATTLE
This rattle is made from a tortoise shell, and was used in healing and fertility rituals by dancers of the Iroquois nation in the eastern woodlands. The noise of rattles was believed to summon spirits to a ritual.

MANDAN MEDICINE
This portrait by artist George Catlin (1794–1872) shows Old Bear, a medicine man of the eastern Plains Mandan tribe. He carries two staffs decorated with furs and feathers, and has healing herbs tucked into the hide around his midriff.

Stylized animal head

BEAKY RATTLE
This elegant carving is a sophisticated rattle that belonged to a shaman of the Tlingit tribe of the Pacific Northwest.

Handle

Jay feathers

White feathers from
a bird of prey

SHAMAN'S HELPER
This headdress was worn
by a Tlingit shaman from the Pacific
Northwest. It represents a guardian
spirit, which was believed to assist
the shaman in driving out evil.

*Mask is in the
form of an eagle face*

Horsehair

CRAZY FACE
Made by the Iroquois people,
this mask was worn in
dances performed by a
group called the "False
Face Society," whose
rituals were believed
to drive off illness
and other sorts of
misfortune.

**DANCE
MASK**
This wooden
Inuit mask
from King
Island, in the
Bering Strait
off the coast of
Alaska, may
represent a bear
or wolf spirit.
Alternatively, it may
simply be a monstrous
spirit-face worn to drive
away evil forces.

*Wolf-like
fangs*

*Masks
characterized
by grimacing or
comical expressions*

At one with nature

Native North American magic-makers traditionally looked to their environment to provide the raw materials – herbs, stones, shells, feathers, bones, and so on – for making remedies, tools, and other magical paraphernalia such as charms, costumes, and masks. They believed in the power of nature, and strove to maintain a sense of unity with its unseen forces.

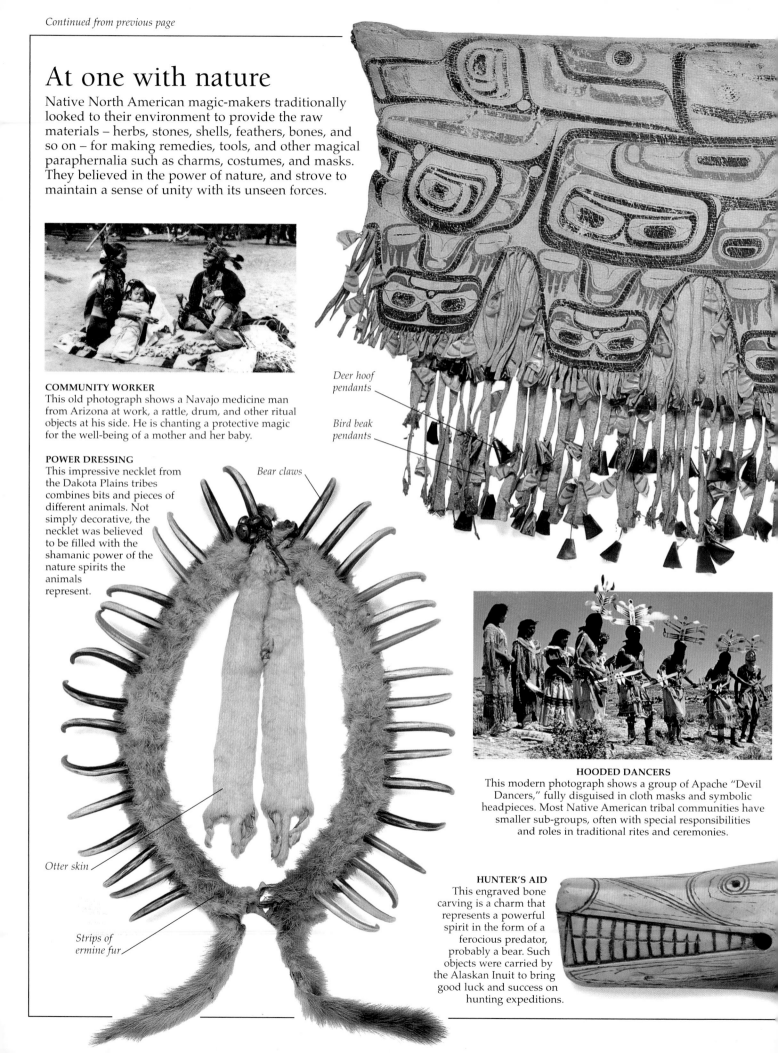

COMMUNITY WORKER
This old photograph shows a Navajo medicine man from Arizona at work, a rattle, drum, and other ritual objects at his side. He is chanting a protective magic for the well-being of a mother and her baby.

POWER DRESSING
This impressive necklet from the Dakota Plains tribes combines bits and pieces of different animals. Not simply decorative, the necklet was believed to be filled with the shamanic power of the nature spirits the animals represent.

Bear claws

Otter skin

Strips of ermine fur

Deer hoof pendants

Bird beak pendants

HOODED DANCERS
This modern photograph shows a group of Apache "Devil Dancers," fully disguised in cloth masks and symbolic headpieces. Most Native American tribal communities have smaller sub-groups, often with special responsibilities and roles in traditional rites and ceremonies.

HUNTER'S AID
This engraved bone carving is a charm that represents a powerful spirit in the form of a ferocious predator, probably a bear. Such objects were carried by the Alaskan Inuit to bring good luck and success on hunting expeditions.

APRON STRINGS
This ceremonial dance-apron was worn by a shaman of the Haida nation on the northwest Pacific coast. Made from animal hide, it is painted with symbolic magical designs. The decorative fringe is hung with pendants that would have rattled during the dance.

Root

Bound paper and muslin packets

Thongs for securing lid

FOR EVERY ILL
To Native Americans, medicine and magic were the same. This shaman's bag from the Dakota Plains Indians held herbs, roots, and other remedies, which would have been ground up and used in medicinal infusions.

Tuft of bear fur represents "hair"

IN THE BOX
This container from the northwest Pacific coast is carved from whalebone in the form of a human head, or perhaps a supernatural being. It probably belonged to a shaman to be used for carrying healing plants and assorted magical objects.

Roughly carved facial features

THE WAY OF THE WARRIOR
In the classic film *A Man Called Horse*, the hero (played by Richard Harris) is hung from a post by claw hooks. This formed part of the Plains Indians' "Sun Dance," an ordeal in which the warrior seeks to glimpse the spirit world and prove his courage.

Figure cut from rawhide

MAGIC TARGETS
These Plains Indian effigies of a warrior and a bison were ritually shot with arrows to bring success in warfare and hunting.

Beyond North America

IN LATIN AMERICA, south of and including Mexico, traditions of magic mingled with religious practices in the great ancient civilizations that once flourished there – the Aztecs of Mexico, with their elaborate rites of human sacrifice; the Mayans of Central America, highly advanced in science as well as divination; the Incas of what is now Peru, with their strange gods and monumental architecture. Today, in these regions, and also in the Caribbean, remarkable forms of magic-making continue, including the eerie rites and sacrifices of *voodoo* in Haiti and the similar practices of *santería* in Brazil and elsewhere. Meanwhile, sorcery and witchcraft on a tribal level – shamanic healing, protection, and so on thrive as much as ever among the peoples of the Amazon forests.

COSTUME JEWELRY
This necklace of engraved animal bones, which would have had a magical as well as a decorative purpose, once belonged to a local village shaman in rural Panama.

Bird effigy

SILVER RAIN
This traditional silver cup was most probably used in healing and rain-making ceremonies. It was owned by a shaman of the Araucanian Indians, whose culture dominated Chile (although it never matched that of the Peruvian Incas) before the Spanish conquest.

Leather seal

SPIRIT HOME
This earthenware jar from Jamaica, called a "govis," jar, was used by a shaman to remove troublesome household spirits. After the spirits were magically trapped inside the jar, it would have been sealed and placed in a corner.

Molded ceramic decoration

Jar is half-filled with sand

BURNING FAITH
This ancient Mayan container is decorated with images of the all-powerful Mayan sun god. It was used to burn incense in rituals that mixed magical and religious elements.

MAGICAL COOKERY
Dating from around 600 A.D., this pottery jar from northern Peru depicts a shaman with a special stick or wand used in the ritual preparation of magical or medicinal substances made from the coca plant.

IN THE BUSH

A lone shaman of the Arara Indians, from the Xingu basin of Amazonia in Brazil, visits the depths of the rain forest to converse with the "monkey spirits." In tribal beliefs, the forest is inhabited by animal and other spirits both good and wicked.

Eye slit

FOREST RATTLE

Made by the Caraja Indians of Brazil, this shaman's rattle consists of a gourd filled with dried beans or seeds. It has simple facial features cut into it, giving it a humanlike quality. Rattles like this were shaken to call the spirits to a ritual, a tradition found in both North and South America.

Mouth

SORCERY FOR SALE

This stall in a "sorcerers' market" in the modern city of La Paz, Bolivia, supplies herbs, powders, ointments, and other ingredients, including the dried bodies of small animals, for magic-making.

CACTUS VISIONS

The mescal, or peyote, cactus, which grows all over Mexico and the southwestern United States, produces a substance – now classed as an illegal drug – that causes hallucinations. It has been widely used by native shamans since Aztec times to induce magical trances and visions.

Earring

VALUABLE OFFERING

This exceptional mask, from the Great Temple in the Aztec capital, Tenochtitlán, was probably created as a magical offering to the gods. It is carved from greenstone with shell and obsidian inlays, and has pierced lobes to support two jade earrings.

Feathers look like hair hanging down from the "head" of the rattle

CAT GOD

This Mayan clay jar bears images of the jaguar, god of the underworld to the Mayans and magically important in many South American religions.

Magical India and Tibet

THE GREAT RELIGIONS OF Hinduism and Buddhism have flourished on the Indian subcontinent for centuries, from Sri Lanka in the south to the Himalayas and Tibet in the north. Popular magical traditions have also been a part of this rich tapestry; in particular, magical charms and amulets, often composed of natural substances, are used as protection against a huge range of evil spirits and other menaces, as well as general ill fortune. Magical practices include a wealth of healing and other rituals, often linked with cults devoted to the warrior goddess Kali. One of the *Vedas* (ancient Hindu sacred hymns) is devoted almost entirely to spells and the detailed rites of magician-priests. Astrology and fortune-telling still provide millions with a guide to daily life, while armies of holy men claim to be experts in divination and the occult.

POPULAR SPIRIT
This ancient terra-cotta plaque depicts a *yakshi* – a type of female nature spirit that could be benign or menacing. Because *yakshis* are featured in many popular folk cults, plaques like this are widespread in India.

Cobra head

HEALING MASK
This traditional wooden mask comes from the island of Sri Lanka. It is carved and painted to represent the serpent demon Garayaka, who was believed to bring about many illnesses by disturbing the body's inner energy balance. A local shaman, in treating a sick client, would have worn the mask in a "purification" ritual to exorcise, or drive out, the evil spirit from the body.

Kali's sword, or "khorgo"

FIERCE DEITY
This ivory carving from West Bengal depicts the goddess Kali, wearing her trademark necklace of severed heads. One of the fiercest of the Hindu gods, Kali shook the earth itself after killing a mighty demon. Many beliefs associate her with witchcraft.

WISE WORDS
This 18th-century Indian painting shows a king and his retinue listening to a wise sage, Sukadeva – who was sometimes considered to be semi-divine – reciting from an epic poem sacred to Hinduism.

FEELING NO PAIN
A common sight in India is of a *fakir* (beggar) lying on a bed of nails or thorns, or perhaps standing on nails, as here. Although far removed from the more magically accomplished *sadhus* (wise men), fakirs demonstrate the amazing, quasi-magical power of the human mind to conquer bodily pain and avoid injury.

DEMON DRAMA
A Tibetan Buddhist monk, or *lama*, wearing a demon-painted mask and colorful costume, plays the part of an evil spirit in a ritual dance-drama based on pre-Buddhist traditions, in which evil is noisily driven out and good finally triumphs. Dances are also designed to magically purify the ground for a forthcoming Buddhist ceremony.

Flames of purifying fire

Skull is a reminder of human mortality

MARKET MAGIC
In a modern town in India, a vendor in a street market offers magical wares – mostly animal parts, including bones, skulls, horns, claws, shells, and more – for healing, as amulets, or for do-it-yourself spell-casting. Such magic merchants can be seen in markets all over the subcontinent.

HIGHLY CHARGED
A double-ended *vajra*, from Tibet, is carried in rituals or while meditating, or is incorporated into other magical tools to "charge" them with magic power.

SACRED HEADGEAR
This ornate headdress, part of a costume worn by a shaman in a Tibetan dance ritual, dates back to the "Bon-po" form of religious worship that existed in Tibet before the advent of Buddhism. Such dances are still performed to drive away demons and appeal to good spirits for healing or protection.

MAGIC DAGGER
This ceremonial implement from Tibet is called a *phur-bu*. It is used symbolically in shamanic rituals, often as a pointer to gather and direct magical energy.

Chin strap

PEELING AWAY
A Tibetan ritual "flaying" knife, used in magical ceremonies as a symbol of the need to strip away the false and superficial "skin" of personal identity, before trying to seek enlightenment.

RITUAL RHYTHMS
A double-sided "skull drum" from Tibet, made from real human skulls and skin, and used in rituals to symbolize the duality (good/evil, day/night, etc.) of the world. As it is twisted, the hanging bead strikes each side alternately.

Southeast Asian magic

SOUTHEAST ASIA BOASTS a remarkable range of peoples and cultures, from remote aboriginal groups to stylish city-dwellers enjoying the high-tech economic boom of extremely prosperous countries such as Singapore. All these cultures provide just as many startling contrasts in their magical practices – these range from the basic, traditional spells, rites, and protections to be found among the tribal people of Java, Borneo, and elsewhere, to more sophisticated forms such as Malaysian divination, Thai shamanism, and Balinese dance ceremonies. Also, in Southeast Asia as in so many other lands, the supernatural forms a spectacular partnership with art – especially in the abundance of wonderful carvings and masks, and including the use of delicate "shadow puppets," originally created for a unique form of magical theater.

Characteristic wild, staring eyes

Demon faces terrify the enemy

FIENDISH FACE
This carved demon mask was used in magical rites on the island of Bali in Indonesia. Sometimes in Southeast Asia such masks are used to frighten off demons, but more often they are worn as part of costumes representing demons in dances that dramatize mythological stories.

Fangs add to monstrous, demonic appearance

SAD IMAGE
A shaman or wizard in present-day Thailand holds up a tiny effigy of a stillborn infant wrapped in red cloth. It is not an eerie reminder for the child's family, but in fact one of the most potent good-luck amulets known in Thai magic-making.

TROUBLE AHEAD
This 19th-century shield, with its disturbing demon faces, was the property of a Kayan headhunter in Borneo. The heads of enemies were taken as trophies to give the hunter status, and as talismans to bring good fortune. The victims were believed to serve as the hunter's slaves in the afterlife.

Bands of human hair increase the shield's power

BANISHING EVIL
This carved and painted wooden image from
Malaysia is a winged female spirit called a
"didouri," which is typically hung in houses
as a magical protection. She carries a comb
to "comb out" evil influences and
a mirror to "reflect" evil energy
and spirits away, including
wicked behavior within
the household.

Comb

Mirror

ALL DRESSED UP
This tribal medicine man
from Java is standing on the
steps of his home, which is
raised off the ground, like
many homes in rural
villages in Southeast Asia.
He carries a staff and is
wearing full ceremonial
body paint and an exotic
feathered headdress, ready
to perform one of the many
rituals from his store of
secret knowledge.

MONSTER MASKS
These ceremonial dancers
from East Kalimantan in
Indonesia gather in a
variety of elaborately
carved and decorated
masks for what is known
as the "hudog" dance – a
typically Southeast Asian
blending of mythical
drama, entertainment
spectacle, and magic ritual.

HOT FEET
A splendidly costumed dancer performs the
famous fire-dance across red-hot coals in
Bali. This ritual displays the dancer's magical
mastery over his own physical senses and
over the element of fire.

Magic in the Far East

CHINA IS ONE of the world's oldest civilizations, and magic-making is deeply entrenched among elements of mysticism, religion, and art. Indeed, Chinese literature on magic is enormous, a strong feature being the occult properties of plants and herbs, as well as clairvoyance and astrology. Wizards and witches (known as *Wu*) were officially recognized even in antiquity. And these magical leftovers, especially the arts of divination, still flourish in modern China. Similarly, aspects of traditional magic thrive in Japan, where the magical arts are recorded in the *Engishiki*, which describe the rituals and spells of priest-magicians 1,000 years ago. Other Far Eastern lands also still retain traditional magicians, who do not seem out of place amid the modern cultural elegance and high-tech wizardry.

SORCERY SESSION
This engraving depicts a gathering of Chinese sorcerers. They have brought their usual equipment of staffs, magic books, and other implements, and are accompanied by rabbits, which are traditionally associated with the moon and with occult matters.

MAGIC REFLECTORS
Since ancient times in China, mirrors have been thought to reveal hidden truths, and to detect and drive away demons. They were often engraved with images of spirits and mysterious astrological symbols. This bronze mirror dates from the third century B.C.

SACRED DISKS
Holed disks of jade or stone, symbolizing heaven, were used in ancient China as amulets and in rites of human sacrifice. Buried with the dead for protection in the afterlife, the jade itself was thought to hold magic power.

DEEP CONTEMPLATION
This Chinese diviner is studying a compass called the *Lo Pan*, used in the ancient magical art of *feng-shui*, which seeks guidance for the positioning of structures in the patterns of mystic forces covering the surface of the earth.

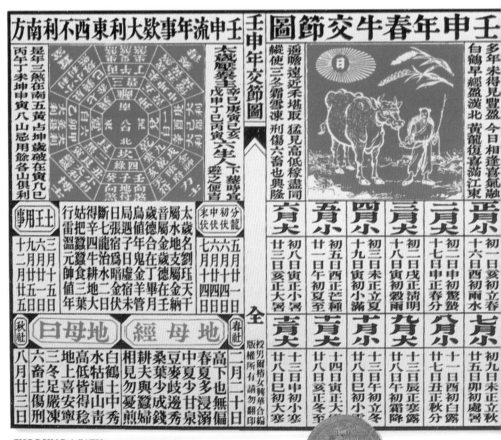

CHOOSING A PATH
An example of a *feng-shui* compass (left) and a "spring cow" chart from an ancient Chinese almanac called the *T'ung Shu*. The diviner would be able to identify from the different characters the various "paths," or courses of action, open to his client.

TOSS A COIN
Among the many forms of simple divination used in China today are these "casting coins." Alternatives include throwing beans or yarrow stalks.

orns give mask
a animalistic
uality

Gruesome features

FUTURE FORETOLD
Fortune-tellers are constantly in demand in Japan, where they act as diviners and suppliers of charms, as well as exorcisers of demons. Here a country woman is consulting a fortune-teller at a temple in Kyoto.

TEMPLE MASK
This Japanese mask might appear to be as frightening as any ceremonial demon mask, but it is in fact a protective spirit face, suspended over the entrance to a Shinto (the official religion of Japan) temple to drive away evil forces.

MONSTER MASK
This richly decorated magical mask from Korea, representing the face of a mad demon, would have been hung in a temple or worn in ceremonies to express the timeless conflict between supernatural forces of good and evil.

ETERNAL OPPOSITES
The *yin-yang* symbol, central to much Chinese mysticism and the Taoist religion (which incorporates many magical elements), symbolizes the universal opposites (good/evil, male/female, light/dark) that must be brought into balance for perfect harmony to exist.

TALISMANIC IMAGE
This maze-like Taoist design, on the lid of a red-and-black lacquer box from 16th-century China, represents the harmonious union of heaven and earth, and is dominated by the character *shou*, which means "long life." Any object inscribed with this character (a popular birthday gift) was considered to be a powerful, life-prolonging talisman for its owner.

Border is decorated with dragon-and-cloud design

Pacific magic

ALTHOUGH THE MANY far-flung island peoples of the South Pacific – including Polynesians, Melanesians, Micronesians, and the Maoris of New Zealand – have differing ideas about gods, spirits, and the supernatural world in general, they have many magical practices in common, especially those relating to island life. Inevitably, the sea plays an important role in magic-making; there are spells for ensuring and improving the fishermen's catches, and exotic shells are used as charms to bring good fortune. Meanwhile, isolated for thousands of years, the Aboriginal peoples of Australia developed their own unique witcheries – in particular, some chilling methods of magical execution – as well as the concept of the "Dreamtime," the era of creation, when ancestral beings traveled across the country giving it its present form.

UNHEALTHY FIBER
This sorcerer's magical implement, which looks like a fly whisk, comes from Murray Island in Torres Strait off Australia. It is said to have enough lethal power to bring about the death of an enemy.

Braided vegetable fiber

WIZARD-IN-CHIEF
This village chief from Papua New Guinea is dressed in ceremonial costume and feathered headdress. Like many local leaders throughout the South Pacific, he is also a practicing sorcerer.

CANNIBAL TREE
Found in Fiji and dating to the 18th century, this extraordinary object is a section of tree trunk with human shinbones hammered through it. It certainly had a magical purpose, probably for protection, and may be evidence of the existence of cannibalism on the island.

CANOE FIGUREHEAD
This carved wooden figure of a god or kindly spirit is from the Solomon Islands. It would once have been fixed to the prow of a seagoing canoe to ward off evil magic and ill luck and to protect the craft and its crew from the perils of dangerous storms.

SACRED COSTUMES
Tribal dancers in grass robes and painted masks are dressed up to represent ancestor spirits, which are venerated by most Pacific islanders.

Spirit figure

IN MEMORY

This carved "malanggan" plaque from New Ireland, an island in the Bismarck Archipelago, is made to commemorate dead relatives. It is used in magical rites and dances that are held one to five years after death occurs. Such carvings are jealously guarded by their owners.

Stingray motif

MAGICAL LURE

This painted stone from Murray Island in Torres Strait was carried to sea in the canoes of fishermen as a talisman to draw fish into their nets.

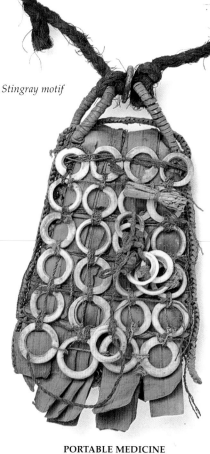

PORTABLE MEDICINE

Like many other tribal peoples, Australian Aborigines believe that disease can be caused by evil sorcery. This "dilly bag" was filled with charms and was carried as a kind of magical health insurance.

Pointing bone

WEATHER POWER

Australian Aboriginal people have combined art and magic in their traditional bark paintings. This example, from Arnhem Land in northern Australia, was used in rain-making ceremonies, with the central image of a stingray as the "watery" power that summons the rain.

DREAM DANCING

This group of Australian Aboriginal men, their bodies painted, are performing a ceremonial dance at a sacred spot. Similar Aboriginal rites are said to allow sorcerers and other special individuals to gain brief access to the spiritual "Dreamtime" and to communicate with the powers residing there.

BITS AND BONES

Tools like these are used by medicine men in northwestern Australia for "good" magic, but longer bones (often with human hair attached), known as "pointing bones," are charged with dire magic to kill anyone they are aimed at.

Polished shell

Modern magic

EVEN IN THE PRESENT day, "magic-making" still survives – in high-tech cities just as much as villages in Africa. It thrives in the rites and ceremonies of a startling assortment of contemporary mystical groups, such as the Druids, and in the "craft" of modern witches, who call themselves "Wicca" (old English for "wise") to escape the association in so many minds of witchcraft with evil. Magic of a sort exists, too, in the "New Age" revival and the search for spiritual meaning in the most ancient traditions and practices, from herbalism and other forms of alternative medicine to the rebirth of shamanism. Astrology is prominent in newspapers and seen on television, and other forms of divination remain popular everywhere. Indeed, most cities have plenty of magic and mystery shops supplying literature, artifacts, and tools for every sort of do-it-yourself witch and wizard.

A simple black or white cord is worn around the waist

MAKING NOISE
This antler rattle, or "singing wand" is used by modern witches to call the spirits in healing rituals. The design echoes longstanding Native American shamanic traditions.

FORMAL DRESS
A robe worn for rituals by a witch of the modern Wicca religion. Sometimes a white robe is preferred, and a colored cord (depending on the ceremony), while a high priestess might wear a more colorful garment. Some groups choose to perform their rites "sky-clad" (naked).

Jangling bells evoke the spirits

HEADY FUMES
Incense burners are widely used in modern magic, just as they have been in the past, when the smoke was thought to carry worshippers' prayers up to the gods.

INCENSE CRYSTALS
One widely used fragrant incense is frankincense, which was also very popular in ancient Egypt.

SACRED CUP
A silver chalice is standard in modern Wicca ceremonies – smaller ones are used when a witch is working alone. In many pagan traditions the magic-maker might sip some liquid as part of a ritual, or pour liquid onto the ground or an altar as a "libation" to the spirits.

EARTH MAGIC
In a modern magical ceremony, a couple works within the confines of a magic circle marked in the ground. The plunging of a sacred knife into the chalice represents the union of masculine and feminine, a ritual performed to gather the power of nature for a magical purpose.

RITUAL BLADE
A carved wood version of the *athame*, the symbolic knife of the Wicca, is used for ritual (non-violent) purposes such as inscribing a magic circle in the ground to gather spiritual power.

Translucent crystal

COILING WAND
A healing wand made from a vine that once twisted around a tree branch, symbolizing the serpent that coiled around the staff of Asclepios, the ancient Greek god of healing.

Hollow tusk contains dried seeds or tiny pebbles

CELTIC SURVIVAL
Robed Druids in Brittany, France, celebrating the summer solstice. Druidic rites and beliefs, which are based on pre-Christian Celtic practices, are very much alive today, especially in Celtic regions like Brittany and Wales.

Turkey feather

RITUAL PERCUSSION
This modern shamanic rattle made from a hollow horn is used together with drums and other instruments to make noise and summon the spirits to a ritual.

OLD SMOKE
This "New-Age" incense stick, called a "smudging stick", is made of sage, cedar, sweetgrass, lavender, and copal (a resin). It is used in rituals for spiritual cleansing.

Insignia worn by high-ranking officer

Red cross symbolizes hidden knowledge of divine nature

FOCUSED POWER
A modern wizard's wand made from a branch and tipped with a large crystal. Crystals of all kinds are believed to collect and store magical energy, focusing it just as prisms focus light. They are used mainly in healing work.

MAGICAL DAWN
This banner and assortment of symbolic badges were used in mystic rites by the Order of the Golden Dawn, a sect founded on ancient principles earlier this century. The group included famous artists, intellectuals, and writers among its ranks, including the Irish poet W. B. Yeats.

Index

Acknowledgments

Dorling Kindersley would like to thank:
Cecil Williamson, Antonia Lovelace, Jim Donne, Elizabeth Carnegie, Sam Scott-Hunter (Assistant to A.W.), Jason Lee, and Julie Ferris.

Additional special photography:
Ellen Howden (Glasgow)

Witch and wizard costume shoot:
Miranda Smith (the witch) and John Laing (the wizard);
Make-up: Jenny Shircore (Tel: 01797 270254); **Prosthetics:** Erin Sherman (Tel: 0181 559 9666);
Witch's hat: supplied by the Unicorn Arts Theatre, Davies Street, London WC2 (Anne Crocker); **Costumes:** supplied by Angels and Bermans, London NW1 (Sally Crees).

Index: Marion Dent

Picture credits
The publisher would like to thank the following for their kind permission to reproduce the images:

(t = top, b = bottom/below, r = right, l = left, c = center, a = above, tl = top left, tr = top right)

AKG London: 15tl, bc, 16br, 21c, 33cr.
The American Museum of Natural History: 27ca.
Ashmolean Museum: 21bl, 50tl.
BFI Stills, Posters & Design: 18cr, br.
The Bridgeman Art Library, London/New York: Christie's, London 38cl; Fitzwilliam Museum 13tl; Giraudon /Louvre, Paris 14tr; Guildhall Art Gallery, Corporation of London 15bl; The De Morgan Foundation, London 17br; Museo Archaeologico, Venice 21cl; National Museum of American Art, Smithsonian /Permlet Art Resource 44cb; Oldham Art Gallery, Lancs. 16br; Palazzo Ducale, Mantua 12br; Collection of the Royal Shakespeare Theatre 17tr; V & A, London 50bc.
The British Museum: 9br, 14b, 20bl, br, tr, cl, c, 21br, t, 33cla, 36tr, 54tr, cr, cl.
Jean-Loup Charmet: 9tr, 19tl, 23cl, 39br.
Corbis UK Ltd.: Bettmann 46tl; JM Dent 19tc.
CM Dixon: 16bl.
Durham Oriental Museum: 31tfl, 55br.
E.T. Archive: 14tl, 37cl, 48bc.
Mary Evans Picture Library: 10c, 12tl, cl, bl, 13tr, c, br, 15cl, 18tl, cr, bl, 19bl, 20cr, 22tr, 23tc, bl, 24tr, br, 26tr, 33cl, clb, 36cr, 54tl.
Exeter Museum: 37tr.

Eye Ubiquitous: John Miles 49tl.
Fortean Picture Library: 13cl, bl, 15tr.
Glasgow Museums: 5tl, 6bla, 7b, 28cra, cl, bl, 29tl, c, bc, cla, 30 cra, c, cb, bla, bl, 31tl, bl, cl, tc, tr, c, cr, cfr, bc, br, 32cfl, 37bla, 40bl, 41cl, 42tfr, tr, tl, c, bl, 42br, 43tr, cr, c, 44cr, l, br, 45bl, 46bl, 46–47t, 47crb, 48c, 49c, 50bl, 51bl, 52r, 56t, bc, 57cl, tc, tl, 57br.
The Ronald Grant Archive: Lorimar 18tr.
Robert Harding Picture Library: 53bl.
Hulton Getty: 15cr, br, 36c, 55tc.
Images Colour Library: Charles Walker Collection 17tl, 22c, 30cl, 32cl, tl, cl, 52cl, 54c, bl.
Impact Photos: Caroline Penn 41br, 43cl; INAH 49tr.
Kobal Collection: *Man Called Horse* 47cl; Warner Bros. /*Witches of Eastwick* 19tr; Orion /Warner Bros/*Witches* 17cr; MGM/*Wizard of Oz* 19br.
Courtesy of the London Dungeon: 4tr, 6br, 27tl, 38tr.
Manchester Museum: 20bc, 26c, 29tr.
The Mansell Collection: 10tr.
Mysteries of Albion (PO Box 19, Twyford, Reading RG10 0HZ – Tel: 01734 320461): 6cl, tr, 10l, 58c, bl, bfr, 59t, l, c, cr.
National Museum of Scotland: 49bc.
Peter Newark's Western Americana: 46cr.
Panos Pictures: Jean-Leo Dugast 27cr, 52bl; Matthew Kneale 51tr; Roderick Johnson 50br; Eric Miller 11tl, 37bl; Cliff Venner 51tl.
Courtesy of The Peabody Essex Museum, Salem, Mass.: Frank Cousins 25bl; Jeffrey Dykes 24bl; Mark Sexton 25r; From the Records of the Court of Oyer and Terminer, 1692,

Property of the Supreme Judicial Court, Division of Archives and Preservation on deposit at the Peabody Museum 24cl.
Photostage: Donald Cooper 25tl.
Pitt Rivers Museum: 40r, 41bc, 48t, 55tl, 56br, 57tr.
Rennes Collection: Dominique M. Camus 8tr.
Rex Features Ltd.: Chat Magazine 58bc; Sipa-Press 59cra.
Royal Pavilion Art Gallery and Museum: 30–31b.
Courtesy of the Royal Shakespeare Company Costume Department, Stratford-upon-Avon: 16–17c.
The Science Museum: Wellcome Collection 29bl, 30cla, 40bc, 41tr, 45br, 50c.
Courtesy of Seven Veils (59 Wickham Avenue, North Cheam, Surrey SM3 8DX – Tel: 0181 644 9529): 58tr.
Smithsonian Institution: 46–47b, 48bl.
South American Pictures: Tony Morrison 49clb.
Statens Historiska Museum: 29bra, br.
Tony Stone: Christopher Arnesen 56bl.
Trip: C. Treppe 42cb; M. Both 53tr; M. Barlow 55tr.
The Witchcraft Research Centre: Cecil Williamson Collection 4tl, cl, cr, br, 5b, 6tl, cr, bc, bl, 8b, br, 10fl, 11br, 22bl, br, 23tl, tr, br, cr, 26l, bl, 26–27b, 27tr, c, 28tr, cr, clb, 29tc, cr, cl 30ca, tr, bc, 31bl, 33tr, cra, tl, br, 36br, 36–37t, 37c, 39tl, 40bc, 41tr, 48br, 51c, cr, br, 53tl.
Walsall Museum and Art Gallery: Gary Kirkham 32bc.
Jerry Young: 38cb, bl.
Zefa Picture Library: 10bc, 40tl, 53br; David Holdsworth 56cl; D. Baglin 57bl.

DK EYEWITNESS BOOKS

SUBJECTS

HISTORY

AFRICA

ANCIENT CHINA

ARMS & ARMOR

BATTLE

CASTLE

COWBOY

EXPLORER

KNIGHT

MEDIEVAL LIFE

MYTHOLOGY

NORTH AMERICAN INDIAN

PIRATE

PRESIDENTS

RUSSIA

SHIPWRECK

TITANIC

VIKING

WITCHES & MAGIC-MAKERS

ANCIENT WORLDS

ANCIENT EGYPT

ANCIENT GREECE

ANCIENT ROME

AZTEC, INCA & MAYA

BIBLE LANDS

MUMMY

PYRAMID

THE BEGINNINGS OF LIFE

ARCHEOLOGY

DINOSAUR

EARLY HUMANS

PREHISTORIC LIFE

THE ARTS

BOOK

COSTUME

DANCE

FILM

MUSIC

TECHNOLOGY

BOAT

CAR

FLYING MACHINE

FUTURE

INVENTION

SPACE EXPLORATION

TRAIN

PAINTING

GOYA

IMPRESSIONISM

LEONARDO & HIS TIMES

MANET

MONET

PERSPECTIVE

RENAISSANCE

VAN GOGH

WATERCOLOR

SCIENCE

ASTRONOMY

CHEMISTRY

EARTH

ECOLOGY

ELECTRICITY

ELECTRONICS

ENERGY

EVOLUTION

FORCE & MOTION

HUMAN BODY

LIFE

LIGHT

MATTER

MEDICINE

SKELETON

TECHNOLOGY

TIME & SPACE

SPORT

BASEBALL

FOOTBALL

OLYMPICS

SOCCER

SPORTS

ANIMALS

AMPHIBIAN

BIRD

BUTTERFLY & MOTH

CAT

DOG

EAGLE &
BIRDS OF PREY

ELEPHANT

FISH

GORILLA,
MONKEY & APE

HORSE

INSECT

MAMMAL

REPTILE

SHARK

WHALE

HABITATS

ARCTIC & ANTARCTIC

DESERT

JUNGLE

OCEAN

POND & RIVER

SEASHORE

THE EARTH

CRYSTAL & GEM

FOSSIL

HURRICANE &
TORNADO

PLANT

ROCKS & MINERALS

SHELL

TREE

VOLCANO &
EARTHQUAKE

WEATHER

THE WORLD AROUND US

BUILDING

CRIME & DETECTION

FARM

FLAG

MEDIA &
COMMUNICATIONS

MONEY

RELIGION

SPY

Future updates and editions will be available online at www.dk.com

DK EYEWITNESS BOOKS

A–Z

DK EYEWITNESS BOOKS

1–110

Future updates and editions will be available online at www.dk.com